Praise For
Beware The Slow Leaks

"After working with Church leaders for over twenty years, I have observed that they have some of the most challenging jobs on the planet. Pastor King articulates slow leaks for which leaders must be attentive and must proactively address to survive and thrive in life and ministry. The ministry environment seems to demand more time, preparation and emotional investment in people, often leading to exhaustion and sometimes to cutting corners and failures. The Word of God provides guardrails to prevent this, but not in the specific context of a contemporary church leader. Pastor King has reflected upon his four decades of pastoral ministry leadership and provided an exegesis in eight practical, thoroughly researched, easily readable chapters. The Gospel-centered principles in *Beware the Slow Leaks* should be on every Christian minister's essential reading list to finish well in the work God has laid out for us."

 —HOWIE LEVIN, executive director,
 OneHeartDC

"Steve King is uniquely equipped to address the difficulties of ministry. He has served with distinction for over thirty-five years and is a role model for all the pastors in the Washington, D.C. area. He is loved by his congregation and respected by ministers from every Gospel-preaching denomination or ethnicity. I commend this book to all believers who are actively attempting to live out the Great Commission."

—**DALE SUTHERLAND**, lead pastor,
McLean (Virginia) Bible Church

"Steve King doesn't trade in easy answers. His struggles, disappointments, and self-deceptions are real—and personal. He doesn't run from them (at least not for long) but chooses to let God teach him through them. What emerges are grounded biblical truths applied in the everyday of life and leadership. Steve has 'practiced what he preaches,' and I am challenged by the graciously delivered truths that he shares. There are no easy outs for those of us on the receiving end of these lessons either. Those are the heart deceits that lead to disaster, and Steve's deep desire is to equip us to see through to the truth that can set us free."

—**DAVID ERICKSON**, president/CEO, ECHO

"In *Beware the Slow Leaks*, Steve King offers urgent, timely, and inspiring biblical wisdom for Christian leaders who want to start strong, thrive fully, and finish well! It's a vital read for today's ministry leaders."

—**W. SCOTT BROWN**, vice president
of Leadership Experiences and Resources,
Christian Leadership Alliance

"Steve King's wisdom, wit and, refreshing transparency make *Beware the Slow Leaks* a necessary practical tool for leaders in any industry. The high-impact life of the leader creates a need for personal self-care, and the principles of this book give effective guidance. This book is a must for every leader who desires to stand the test of time!"

—**DR. BOBBY MANNING**, senior pastor,
First Baptist Church of District Heights (Maryland)

"Every pastor wakes up one day and wants to quit. Learning how to configure your life and ministry for the long run is key. Having personally been mentored by Steve, I can tell you that the concepts and wisdom in this book are indispensable for enduring in your call."

—**JASON CONNER**, lead pastor,
Portico Church, Arlington, Virginia

"If I were asked for contemporary examples of finishing strong, Steve King is one of the first Christian leaders that would come to my mind. I will never forget him shocking our church by announcing during one of his own sermons that he had concluded we needed a new pastor—and that he believed God was calling him to become that new pastor. Twenty years later, I can testify that is exactly what God enabled Steve to do. When most leaders would have been coasting and leaking, he was humbling himself and growing. He has not only managed his own leaks but has played a significant role in helping me to manage mine."

—**DAVE LYONS**,
international vice president,
The Navigators

"As I was reading this book, my mind flashed back to the late 1980s when I was an intern at Cherrydale Baptist Church and later, when my fiancée and I were going through premarital counseling with our pastor, Steve King. Several of the godly principles contained in this book we heard in counseling thirty years ago, and they have stayed with us and blessed us immeasurably throughout our marriage and ministries.

"This book is not about Steve King. It is about the God of grace and peace bringing Steve and Mae King through a multitude of trials, teaching them godly principles for growing healthy relationships, and sharing those principles with others."

—**JEFF SANDERS**, executive director of Operations
for Ohio and Western Pennsylvania,
Marketplace Chaplains

"I met Steve at the 100 Cities Conference in Washington, D.C. in November 2018, and our hearts were instantly knit together. He writes in this book that 'not seeking out authentic friendships is going against the way God designed you.' I totally agree! In fact, not aligning with John 17 in every set of relationships, from family to friendships to the city Church and beyond, is at best failing to align with Jesus's own heartbeat.

"Steve is both a practitioner and an excellent and creative writer. This will be another must-have for pastors and ministry leaders everywhere."

—**DAVE DRUM**, founder,
J17 Ministries, Tucson, Arizona

"I wholeheartedly recommend Steve's extraordinary book. It is full, from cover to cover, with godly wisdom and counsel for all who want to walk a Gospel-centered and grace-filled life. He helps us all understand what it means to walk through every day with Jesus Christ."

—**BRIAN WEBSTER**, senior pastor,
Christ Church of Arlington (Virginia)

"I have known Pastor King for twenty years, and during that time, it has been my privilege to be a part of his 'band of brothers' that he writes about in Chapter Seven. This has allowed me a front-row seat to watch him apply these eight principles to his life and put a plug in the slow leaks. This book is filled with valuable wisdom that will help you finish strong."

—**JOHN SLYE**, senior pastor,
Grace Community Church,
Arlington, Virginia

"Bottom line: It is awesome. Lifted my head above the clouds, lifted my perspective, and left me walking away optimistic and rejuvenated, knowing the Lord lives, is good, and good to me. Timeless and phenomenal analogies provide the reader with powerful tools to live a godly life."

—**FIRST LIEUTENANT RANDOLPH CAREY**,
Officer In Charge, Analysis,
Correlation and Fusion Cell,
613th Air Operations Center,
Pacific Air Force

"Not a month goes by I don't hear a story of pastoral burnout, ministry failure, or moral compromise. Sadly, it's far more common to hear of a pastor who quits, fails, or falls than it is to hear of a pastor finishing a long and fruitful ministry with dignity. Steve King is one such man. For decades, he has given himself to his sheep and also to other shepherds. Pastors all over the District of Columbia have stories of a time when Steve helped them out of a slump or encouraged them through a particularly brutal season of ministry. The insights of this book are a powerful and preventive message for every pastor who desires to hear 'well done' at the finish line."

> —**CLINT CLIFTON**, author of *Church Planting Thresholds: A Gospel-Centered Guide*, North American Mission Board, director of Send DC

"Too often technique and numeric growth are on the minds of young pastors. Learn from a veteran and seek faithfulness!"

> —**MATT SCHMUCKER**, co-founder, 9Marks

BEWARE THE SLOW LEAKS

BEWARE
THE SLOW
LEAKS

Eight Ways
Ministry Leaders Can Thrive
and Finish Strong

STEVE KING

SALEMBOOKS
an imprint of Regnery Publishing

Regnery® is a registered trademark of Salem Communications Holding Corporation

Salem Books™ is a trademark of Salem Communications Holding Corporation

Cataloging-in-Publication data on file with the Library of Congress

ISBN: 978-1-62157-812-3
Ebook ISBN: 978-1-62157-903-8

Published in the United States by
Salem Books, an imprint of Regnery Publishing
A Division of Salem Media Group
300 New Jersey Ave NW
Washington, DC 20001

www.Regnery.com

Manufactured in the United States of America

2019 Printing

Books are available in quantity for promotional or premium use. For information on discounts and terms, please visit our website: www.Regnery.com

I often say, "I have Jesus and Mae Belle. I am a blessed man."

This book is dedicated to Jesus Christ, Who authored and is perfecting my faith, and Mae Belle, my sweetheart who has faithfully walked beside me as the truths of this book were deposited into our lives.

Contents

Introduction

No one suddenly experiences a moral blowout. The demise of our decency is always preceded by unwise decisions that function like slow leaks.

Yet there is hope. Jesus Christ longs to instill grace-sourced essentials in our lives—essentials that will plug our punctures and enable us to flourish and finish well.

Many years ago, when I was starting out in ministry, I deeply admired the senior pastor of a nearby church. I was not the only one who was captured by his love for people, courageous leadership, authenticity, compelling sermons, vibrant marriage, and hard-earned wisdom. His growing congregation loved him because he passionately loved them. He earned their trust by humbly and faithfully leading them from a place of debt, decline, and division to financial stability, growth, and unity in Christ. He taught them how to be authentic by sharing openly about his battle with depression. When their worship pastor was found to be sexually involved with women in the congregation, he taught his confused flock how to exercise restorative church discipline. He fed them from God's Word, confronted sin at its roots, labored with faithful teams, and led the way toward restoration. Over a period of several years, deep repentance and healing spread through the church family. An amazing story unfolded that resulted in many healed marriages and the fallen worship pastor's eventual restoration.

This faithful shepherd taught and modeled how to share the Gospel winsomely—every year, more than a hundred new converts were baptized and joined the growing church family. His influence on aspiring leaders grew as he trained a steady stream of interns. He became my mentor during my first two years as a pastor, and I was delighted when he agreed to deliver the keynote address at my ordination service. His charge to me still replays in my mind: "Steve, love, lead, and feed. Consistently love people, lead them to Christ, and faithfully feed them God's Word."

Ten years later, I was pastoring my second church on the other side of the country from my mentor. I longed for my new church family to experience the man who had so positively marked my life. I was delighted when he agreed to deliver the keynote address at our churchwide retreat.

As our team prayed and prepared for it, the first signs of a possible "slow leak" in my hero's walk with God began to emerge. The young woman in our congregation who arranged his travel plans told me he was extremely demanding and off-putting. I wrote it off as a misunderstanding because she was a relatively new believer and I had never heard anyone speak about him that way.

His messages at the retreat impacted me and our church family the way I hoped they would. However, over the weekend, my mentor was strangely distant and always found an excuse to scurry away and not engage me and others. I was hurt and confused. Several weeks later, I discovered he was engaged in an affair. He divorced his wife and left the ministry.

That devastating disappointment put the fear of God in me: "Let him who thinks he stands take heed lest he fall" (1 Corinthians 10:12). Yet, as I was later to learn, my mentor did not abruptly experience a "blowout." His failure was preceded by dozens of unattended "slow leaks" in his walk with God.

No one suddenly has a moral blowout. The demise of our decency is *always* preceded by unwise decisions that function like slow leaks. God wants us to beware the slow leaks, and He has provided all we need to make this possible. Yet even what appears to be a catastrophic blowout need not be permanent! The other side of the coin of "beware the slow leaks" is to "behold the Ultimate Leak-Minder," even after a major blowout. God's grace-sourced essentials can restore the fallen so they can indeed flourish and finish well. Keep reading: My mentor was restored, and so was his marriage!

THE AIM OF THIS BOOK

I don't just want to finish strong in my life and ministry; I want to thrive along the way! The two cannot be separated any more than we can separate loving God from loving people. The fact that you are reading this book may indicate you have the same hopes. How can we both flourish and finish well?

I have discovered eight grace-sourced essentials, gleaned from over forty years of in-the-trenches pastoral ministry. These essentials have prevented me from losing heart thousands of times! They have taught me how to cooperate with Jesus Christ in spotting and plugging the slow leaks in my character. My ultimate hope is not in the insights I have gained or the essentials I am pursuing but in the grace of God that flows from the author and perfecter of our faith, Jesus Christ (Hebrews 12:2). Therefore, I am inviting you on a journey to evaluate and revitalize *your* reliance on God's grace as you read this book.

Each chapter explores tried and tested *essentials* for Christian leaders to thrive and finish strong. These essential *ways of the Lord* have been available to generations of God's people. Trace the phrase "the way" through the Bible, and you will discover the following:

- God chose Abraham to keep *the way of the Lord* (Genesis 18:19).
- Moses and David pleaded, "Let me know your *ways*, O Lord." (Exodus 33:13; Psalm 25:4).
- Moses repeatedly exhorted Israel to walk in *God's ways* by fearing Him, loving Him, clinging to His commands, and singing of his ways. He tells them *God's ways* are pleasant, good, righteous and everlasting (Deuteronomy 8–10; 26–28).
- John the Baptist came to prepare *the way of the Lord* (Matthew 3:3).
- Jesus took all the threads of *God's ways*, pulled them into Himself, and said, "*I am the way*, and the truth, and the life; no one comes to the Father but through Me" (John 14:6).

No wonder early Christians were called followers of *the way* (Acts 9:2; 19:9, 23; 24:22). Jesus Christ is on duty 24/7, 365 to complete the good work He began in us and to bring us home intact (Philippians 1:6; Romans 8:28–29). Yet His essential *ways* are not for passive bystanders; instead, they are for those who are alert to His grace-call.

OVERVIEW OF OUR JOURNEY

We will begin our journey by facing reality: There are only two ways to live. These alternatives were permanently imprinted on my psyche in a shocking way, and I am eager to pass it along to you. You will learn why *checking your filter* is the first essential to flourishing and finishing well.

In Chapter Two, we'll learn to be shaped by the Gospel. This is core to flourishing and finishing well, as well as an essential discipline for all spiritual leaders. We will discover why the Gospel must be central, and I'll equip you with two tools that will help you and those you lead to move from "living on the surface" to experiencing change from the heart. Do you find yourself swinging like a pendulum between pride over your progress to despair over your failures? Do you often feel superior or inferior to others? We will discover how to escape that ugly cycle and replace it with lasting change from a heart-Gospel interchange.

In Chapter Three, we'll discuss how Jesus Christ is fulfilling His redemptive and restorative purposes through people, and His sovereign rule means that He accomplishes His purposes through both those who belong to Him *and those who do not* (John 19:11; Acts 2:23; Luke 19:10; Matthew 28:18–20). However, Jesus is *directly* working through His people as they fulfill their unique callings (Ephesians 2:10; Colossians 3:23; 1 Corinthians 10:31). As all believers are part of the body of Christ, we will focus specifically on Jesus's promise that He would build His church (1 Corinthians 12:13; Matthew 16:18). We will discover the core essentials of what a healthy church is and align our lives with what Jesus is building. The church is His major leak-mending tool in our lives!

The fourth chapter is designed to help you come to terms with an often-overlooked truth: God is extravagant in His grace *and* extensive in His discipline. We will explore what it means to *let the grace of God instruct us*, and we'll uncover compelling motivations tucked away in the five warning passages of the New Testament book of Hebrews.

Chapter Five connects thriving in leadership with a healthy marital relationship. The principle of constantly rekindling the marriage flame is rooted in convictions built around God's definition of marriage and wise choices empowered by the Holy Spirit.

Chapter Six will help you determine your leadership path. Are you a leader people want to follow? Are you multiplying leaders? We will look at leadership by contrasting the selfish leadership of King Herod and the servant leadership of Jesus Christ. Heeding Jesus's grace-call to lead us as we lead others will radically alter the way we handle criticism, cast vision, stay motivated, and empower others.

Chapter Seven explores the value of a band of brothers who can help you learn the wisdom of teamwork, the value of a high-trust culture, and the power of a Kingdom mindset. So many leaders are lonely and long for a band of brothers This chapter will show you how to find your band.

In Chapter Eight, we'll discover how Jesus restored two men whose names are associated with doubt and denial. Our discovery will show us how to incorporate grace-sourced habits into our lives that will prevent us from losing heart. This essential will empower you to crash through your quitting points.

Let's begin the journey!

CHAPTER 1

Check Your Filter

"There is no such thing as not worshiping. Everybody worships."

—David Foster Wallace

There once was a man in my life that I have always thought of as a "branding iron" because, in one short exposure, he permanently marked me. That's leadership! His tattoo on my psyche came unexpectedly in the form of a question. He simply asked, "Isn't God good?"

The circumstances surrounding his question and the tone in which he delivered it pried open a place deep inside me and rubbed the raw edge of my faith. Little did I know he was about to implant in me the most constructive insight about what it means to truly trust God. His example would deposit truth in me which has become a treasure chest I have drawn from for over forty years. I have passed its riches on to countless others and seen it fortify their faith as well. It is the first essential to flourishing and finishing well, especially for leaders.

I met the man, heard his story, and was asked his probing question when Mae Belle and I arrived on the West Coast as newlyweds. Our honeymoon consisted of driving across the nation from our hometown of Atlanta, Georgia, to Western Seminary in Portland, Oregon. A "big brother" upperclassman named Tom Heflin had been assigned to me as a mentor and to help me adjust to seminary life. Mae and I settled into our new apartment, and I gave Tom a call. He immediately made me feel welcome. We exchanged enough information to get acquainted and made plans to get together a few days later.

Just as we were about to hang up, he said, "Steve, did you hear what happened to me this weekend?" I said, "No, I just arrived in town and have not spoken to anyone else." He then told me his shocking story.

He said, "I work in a warehouse with several other seminary students. We were shutting down the plant for the weekend, and I was in the back of the facility cleaning a machine. My right arm was fully extended into the device I was cleaning. The other men were in the front of the plant and did not know I was in the back. One of them flipped a switch, which activated the machine I was refurbishing; my right arm was immediately cut off just below the shoulder. I arrived home from the hospital today." He then paused and said, "Isn't God good?"

His tone was not cynical or flippant but reverent and trusting. I was stunned. "What did you say?" I asked. "Tell me again what you said happened to you." He patiently relayed the story, adding a few more details, and then ended with the same question, "Isn't God good?" He did not pose it as a question he wanted me to answer but as a core creedal conviction he was inviting me to embrace with him.

His question uncovered my skepticism. I wondered, *Is he in shock? Is he mouthing spiritual platitudes to impress me as his "little brother" in the seminary?* Then I thought, *Maybe he knows God in a way I do not know Him. Perhaps he has learned something about trusting God in the face of devastating loss that I have never tasted.* At that moment, I determined to closely examine this man's life. If his faith was real, I wanted what he had. I expressed my concern for him, prayed for him, and hung up the phone.

Over the next several years, I watched him walk with God in all sorts of settings. Tom declared openly his compassion and forgiveness to the co-worker who had flipped the switch and ripped off his arm. He constantly reassured that brother, declaring "God is good and can be trusted in spite of our circumstances." His leadership taught me how trusting God spills over to how we treat people.

He worked his way through rehab and all the hard adjustments of learning to live with a prosthetic arm. I can still picture him maneuvering his "prosthetic partner" as he spoke in preaching class, worked in a study group with other students, shuffled papers as he prepared to teach, or helped his wife clean up after hosting people in their home. He forged his fake arm into a platform to share, in a winsome way, the authentic goodness of God, fully revealed in Jesus Christ. His leadership taught me to connect trusting God with selflessly serving others.

Tom's favorite subject was Jesus. During seminary, he mastered the four gospels and constantly saturated himself with truths about the Savior. He put together a course on the life of Christ and labored over its content. He was captured by Jesus's love for him. I remember him saying with deep passion on countless occasions, "The life of Christ!" Tom was not talking about theological information regarding a religious figure but about the living and loving Savior Who daily shaped his life.

Tom was truly a "big brother" to me during those early years of seminary. He taught me by his example the first essential to flourishing and finishing well as a leader: *Check your filter. There are only two available.*

To help you never forget the lesson he burned into my psyche, please carefully read and follow these instructions:

Fully extend your left arm and lift your hand so you can see all five of your fingers fully extended. Your extended left hand represents your life circumstances, good and bad. Now take your right hand and slightly spread your fingers as if they were a "filter" you could look through. Place your right hand over your eyes, so you can look through the gaps between your fingers. The "filter" formed by the parted fingers of your right hand represents the character and promises of God.

This is the first filter God longs for us to keep in place. Filter your life through the character and promises of God!

I realized that when Tom asked me, "Isn't God good?" after having his arm severed, he was looking through his faith filter. He had been in the habit of constantly feeding his faith through heart-driven study of the life of Christ. As a result, he perceived the tragic loss through the grid of the goodness and trustworthiness of God, fully revealed in Jesus Christ. He learned to measure God's goodness by the cross, not his circumstances! He learned to measure God's power by Jesus's resurrection from the dead, not his own life condition![1]

There is another filter available to us. It is our only other option, and it reverses the order of the first. To help you remember the second filter, please heed the following instructions:

Fully extend your right hand, which represents the character and promises of God, and bring your left hand, which represents your life circumstances, before your eyes, using your fingers as a filter.

This second option is too often the way we live: We filter God through the circumstances of life and, as a result, believe lies about His holy character. We lose heart, and our hearts are hardened.

These two filters on life (let's call them *Filter One* and *Filter Two*) profoundly shape every aspect of our lives. Followers of Christ are called to be "Filter One leaders." Abandon or neglect this call, and you will neither flourish nor finish well. You can take Jesus's word for it (Matthew 7:21–27).

Tom had a profound impact on me and others because he was a Filter One leader. Filter Two leaders have influence, but it is not in the same league as Filter One leaders. Filter One leaders are salt and light while Filter Two leaders are just influencers—and often their "slow leaks" damage their positive influence. Face it: We need to check our filter as leaders and come to terms with reality. There are *only* two options available to us.

THE DIFFERENCE BETWEEN THE FILTERS

Filter One leaders: Filter life through the character and promise of God.

Filter Two leaders: Filter God through the circumstances of life.

The Bible calls the first approach the way of wisdom and worship and the second the way of a fool and idolatry (Proverbs 1:7; 3:5–6; Psalms 14:1; Matthew 22:37–38; 1 Thessalonians 1:9).

Filter One leaders are humble before God and people. They are daily learning to filter life through the character and promises of God. The result is confidence, inner peace, and discernment. The power of God strengthens them, and they are keenly aware of the dangers of Filter Two leadership. "Beware the slow leaks" is their motto!

Filter Two leaders are arrogant before God and people. They daily feed their unbelief by filtering God through the circumstances of life. Therefore, they carry the extra weight that always comes with unbelief: stress, worry, anxiety, and frustration. They may appear to flourish in the short-term, but the slow leaks of unbelief eventually erode their character so they neither flourish nor finish well.

Are you a Filter One or Filter Two leader? Those are your only two options. We are always moving in the direction of one or the other. The issue is not perfection on our part; instead, we look for progression in daily cooperating with Him in looking at life through the lens of His character and promises. Chances are that you long to be a Filter One leader because you are reading this book.

Once you are aware of these two ways of viewing life, you will read the Bible with a new awareness. From beginning to end, the Bible contrasts Filter One and Filter Two leaders: Cain and Abel, Abraham and Lot, Joseph and his brothers, Moses and Pharaoh, Joshua and the leaders of Jericho, Saul and David—and the contrast continues right to the end, with judgment on those who refuse to believe and eternal life for those who hope in God. The redeemed will spend eternity praising God as they forever view their lives through His character and promises.

In addition, observant people down through the ages have awakened to "the only two options" they have: worship or idolatry, Filter One or Filter Two. God never leaves himself without a witness.

For example, David Foster Wallace was considered by many to be one of the most brilliant American writers of his generation. He was a novelist, essayist, and professor of literature at Pomona College in Claremont, California. He is most famous for a commencement speech he gave to graduating students at Ohio's Kenyon College. In it, he describes the reality of idolatry in all our lives and its devastating impact.

This, I submit, is the freedom of a real education, of learning how to be well-adjusted. You get to consciously decide what has meaning and what doesn't. You get to decide what to worship. Because here's something else that's weird but true: in the day-to-day trenches of adult life, there is no such thing as atheism. <u>*There is no such thing as not worshiping. Everybody worships.*</u> *The only choice we get is what to worship.*

. . . If you worship money and things, if they are where you tap real meaning in life, then you will never have enough, never feel you have enough. Worship your body and beauty and sexual allure, and you will always feel ugly. Worship power, you will end up feeling weak and afraid, and you will need ever more power over others to numb you to your own fear. Worship your intellect, being smart, you will end up feeling stupid, a fraud, always on the verge of being found out. <u>*But the insidious thing about these forms of worship*</u> *is not that they're evil or sinful,* <u>*it's that they're unconscious. They are default settings.*</u> *They're the kind of worship you just gradually slip into, day after day, getting more and more selective about what you see and how you measure value without ever being fully aware that that's what you're doing.*[2]

Wallace was seeking to wake these graduates up to the "only two options": God or idolatry. Perhaps his commencement speech is considered one of the best of all time because "the only two options" resonates with what our consciences tell us is true.

Others before Wallace saw the dangers of idolatry, which is at the heart of Filter Two leadership. The French philosopher Simone Weil (1909–1943), who was a mystic, a political activist, and a follower of Jesus Christ, said, "One has only the choice between God and idolatry. There is no other possibility. For the faculty of worship is in us, and it is either directed somewhere into this world, or into another."

Have you ever connected the worship of God or idolatry to leadership? This again is another way of referring to the call to check our filter!

Blaise Pascal (1623–1662), who was a mathematician, physicist, inventor, and theologian, saw the only two options clearly as revealed in his famous statement: "There is a God-shaped vacuum in the heart of each man which cannot be satisfied by any created thing but only by God the Creator, made known through Jesus Christ." Filter One leaders possess an internal satisfaction because they trust God while Filter Two leaders live with the God-shaped vacuum.

Augustine, Bishop of Hippo (354–430 AD), clearly understood we only have two options and declared in his Confessions: "Thou hast made us for thyself, O Lord, and our heart is restless until it finds its rest in thee." Filter One leaders find their rest in God, and Filter Two leaders remain restless.

Have you seriously heeded the reality of the "only two options"? Are you on the path of Filter One leadership?[3] When I pondered those two questions, it led me to face two more even more important ones:

WHY AND HOW?

There are two very important questions we must answer if we want to be progressively marked as Filter One leaders.

Why should we filter life through the character and promises of God? *Why* should we consider this the only wise way to live? *Why* do we need to put God in the center of our thinking?

How do we filter life through the character and promises of God? What does it look like in everyday life?

Jesus Christ is the answer to *both* the why and the how questions. That is good news because the *motivation* we need to keep trusting God is *not* found in a philosophy we must master, a set of precepts we must inculcate, or a bunch of practices we must follow but in a Person Who adores us—Jesus Christ.

Let's walk through some essential truths Filter One leaders must embrace. The more I ponder these truths and let their implications sink in, the more motivated I am to trust God fully. And I believe the same can happen to you.

Let's begin by looking at the *only* person who can equip us to become Filter One leaders. In Jesus Christ, we have the *only* Person Who perfectly filtered all of life through the character and promises of God (Matthew 26:39; Luke 22:42; John 5:17–30). He *alone* can show us the why and the how of it and provide the ongoing motivation we need! He is the author and perfecter of our faith (Hebrews 12:2). All the promises of God are yes in Him (2 Corinthians 1:20). He is the final and complete revelation of God to man (Hebrews 1:1–3). In Him are hidden all the treasures of wisdom and knowledge (Colossians 2:1–3). He is the theme of the Scriptures; every story whispers His name (John 5:39; Luke 24:44)![4]

JESUS IS THE ULTIMATE *WHY*

Jesus is the answer to the ultimate *why* behind everything. Many of us know the answer to the question in the Westminster shorter catechism regarding *man's* chief end: It is to glorify God, and to enjoy him forever (1 Corinthians 10:31; Romans 11:36; Psalm 73:24–26; John 17:22, 24). Yet how many of us have seriously pondered the unstated assumption *behind* man's chief end? What is the chief end of God? Read the next sentence twice and let it sink in!

Only if we know God's chief end can we understand *why* our chief end is to glorify God and enjoy Him forever.

The Bible's answer to God's chief end may surprise and disturb you. However, if you embrace this truth, you will have tapped into *the* motivation to filter all of life through the character and promises of God. It is the rock-solid foundation that a Filter One leader stands upon.

What is number one on God's priority list? What is number two, three, nine, and on till ten thousand? It is always the same answer: God's glory (Isaiah 48:9–11).[5]

Why does the Bible command us to recognize, honor, declare, praise, reflect, and live for God's glory? Because God's passion is to be glorified (Matthew 5:16; 1 Corinthians 10:31).

What is God's motivation behind creation, judgment, answered prayers, healing, sending His Son, sending the Holy Spirit, inspiring the Scriptures, and saving us? It is to glorify Himself (Isaiah 43:6–7; Jeremiah 13:11; John 17:1; 2 Thessalonians 1:9–10).

Are you getting uncomfortable? You may reason this way: For *us* to constantly seek our own glory is the essence of evil and therefore self-destructive (Jeremiah 2:12–13; Romans 1:18–32)! So why is it *wrong for us* to seek our own glory and *right for God* to seek His own glory?

One of the most clarifying answers to that probing question comes from the pen of J. I. Packer in *The Plan of God* (Evangelical Press, 1965):

The reason why it cannot be right for man to live for himself, as if he were God, is simply the fact that he is not God; and the reason why it cannot be wrong for God to seek His own glory is simply the fact that He is God. Those who would not have God seek His glory in all things are really asking that He should cease to be God. And there is no greater blasphemy than to will God out of existence.[6]

Make the connection between God's passion to glorify Himself and the reason Jesus came.

Why did Jesus come? He came to glorify the Father (John 17:1), and His passion to glorify the Father is inseparable from His love *for us* (John 17:23)!

The maximum expression of God's glory is the work of Jesus Christ on *our behalf* (2 Corinthians 3:18–4:6; Philippians 2:10–11; Revelation 5:1–14).

Think about it. God's passion for His glory and His commitment to us in Christ are inseparable.

What was the joy set before Jesus that propelled Him to go to the cross (Hebrews 12:2)? It was the joy of bringing glory to the Father by purchasing *us* with His own blood (1 Peter 1:18–19).

What is the one thing Jesus did not have in Heaven? *He did not have us!* If He did not become a man, live a righteous life, suffer at the hands of sinners, go to the cross to bear our sins, and rise from the dead, He would not have *us*. Only His death in *our* place made it possible for Him to have *us* (1 Peter 3:18).

The fact that God's primary purpose is to glorify himself is exhilarating news because:

- *God's passion for His glory guarantees His unwavering commitment to us* (Philippians 2:1–11).
- *God's passion for His glory always enhances our value and never diminishes it* (Genesis 1:26–28).
- *God's passion for His glory drove Him to remove every barrier preventing us from delighting in Him* (John 3:16–18).
- *God's passion for His glory proves his love for us* (Romans 5:8; 1 John 4:10).

In Jesus Christ *alone* we see the unbreakable link between God's passion for His own glory and God's passionate love for us. Making this connection is the first essential to becoming a Filter One leader. Jesus lays the foundation for this truth by making us aware of a reality we often ignore . . .

Our heart always has a treasure, and we are always mastered by the treasure of our heart.

We are willing to lose almost anything to gain what we consider to be our true treasure. The treasures of our heart drive us. If our heart treasures are threatened, we panic, we get anxious, and we go into defense mode to protect our valuables. That is why we find it *easy* to sacrifice our time, resources, and energy on the most valuable treasures of our heart. Show me how you expend your time, money, and resources, and I will show you the dominant treasures of your heart and the masters you serve.

Therefore, we are all worshipers, and we always will be. Worship comes from the words *worth* and *ship*. It means to ascribe worth, value, and honor to something. We worship the treasures of our heart and bow to these masters. Where do you draw your significance, security, and hope? What is it that makes life worth living for you? What would cause you to say, "If I lose that, life is not worth living?" Your answer reveals your heart treasure and master. These are your *functional* saviors and lords.

Filter One leaders treasure God above *all else*. This is their golden key to flourishing and finishing well. Filter Two leaders treasure cheap substitutes for God, and these blind them to the dangers of their demise.

Jesus Christ, the *ultimate* Filter One leader, enables us to *face the reality* of our need, explains the *why* behind our need, and *motivates* us to walk the path of a Filter One leader. Filter One leaders know the answers to the following questions: What is the treasure of Jesus's heart? What was He willing to lose in order to gain everything?

- To gain *us*, Jesus had to lose the freedom and comfort of Heaven and stoop to become an embryo in Mary's womb (Matthew 1:18).
- To gain *us*, Jesus had to lose intimacy with God the Father: "Why have you forsaken me?" (Matthew 27:45–46).
- To gain *us*, Jesus had to lose His innocence and be treated as a sinner (2 Corinthians 5:21).
- To gain *us*, Jesus had to endure rejection and be crucified as a criminal (Luke 9:23).
- To gain *us*, Jesus had to bear our sins in His body on the cross and be cursed in our place (1 Peter 2:24; Galatians 3:14).

Jesus treasures the Father and *us*. The two are inseparable, as loving God and loving people are inseparable commands (Matthew 22:37–40). For Him, to treasure and love the Father was to treasure and love *us* (John 3:16–18; Luke 19:10).

In Jesus Christ, we have the *why* and the *how* of filtering all of life through the character and promises of God.

When we see Him treasuring us, then we will treasure Him!

This is grace-based motivation. When His love for us captures our hearts, we no longer live for ourselves but for Him Who died and rose again on our behalf (2 Corinthians 5:14–15). This is the how of it. Seeing the glory of God in Christ is what compels us to trust God and filter the circumstances of our lives through His character and promises.

Our greatest need is to see the glory of God in Christ—and when we see it, we trust Him and begin to filter all of life through His character and promises. This is the golden key to Filter One leadership!

WHAT DOES FILTER ONE LEADERSHIP LOOK LIKE?

Because our church is committed to missions and has always given at least 25 percent of its budget to global missions over its 105-year history, our pastors end up connecting with Filter One leaders around the world. My friend Berhanu's life message demonstrates Filter One leadership in the context of great loss. He committed his life to Christ as a teenager in his native Ethiopia and began to share the Gospel with his friends; many embraced the faith. But during his high school days, civil war broke out in his country. He watched as revolutionaries burned his church, murdered his brother, and persecuted those he loved.

He and a friend decided to start over. They hired an evangelist and planted a church in a city park. That small beginning multiplied; today, there are more than four hundred churches in their network, and I have had the joy of training many of their pastors.

Berhanu married a godly woman with whom he had three children. This past year, he lost his wife to cancer, and I have grieved with him countless times. Yet his faith filter is firmly in place. He told me recently, "I have moved from focusing on *why* to trust. I am more in love with the Lord than I have ever been. The truths I run through my mind are 'God is sovereign, God is good, I will trust Him as I should.' My mission is clear—to glorify God by investing in my children and making disciples of Jesus."

In the four decades I have been pastoring, I've had the privilege of knowing many Filter One leaders. These are some of my favorites.

Thirty years ago, a godly young woman in our church was considering dating a young man. She wasn't sure of his commitment to Christ and made clear that the relationship would not continue unless he seriously explored the faith, beginning by meeting with me.

Rob had an attitude because he wanted the girl but did not want to meet with me. He began by folding his arms and communicating why he did not want to follow Christ. His thesis was that people do not change. He gave several examples and zeroed in on a man named Danny who had been the head of the Ku Klux Klan in his area and had done horrible things to him and others. He said, "People like him do not change!"

What Rob didn't know was that Danny was sitting in the next office and was a member of our staff. He had become a Christian, and I had been in a small group with him for several years. He had radically changed.

I asked Rob to excuse me for a moment; I went to the next office and asked Danny to come into mine. I said, "You are a man of God; you will know what to do."

When Danny walked in, Rob was shocked! Danny then shared his conversion story with him and asked Rob to forgive him for the things he had done. Soon after that, Rob became a follower of Christ, married the young lady, and he and Danny became friends. Now, thirty years later, I often see them after one of our worship services, joyfully delighting in Christ together. Rob and Danny have become Filter One leaders, and each one is faithfully passing his influence on to the next generation.

My wife, Mae Belle, is a Filter One leader who has shaped generations of seventh- and eighth-grade students to view life through the lens of God's story of creation, fall, redemption, and restoration in Christ. She learned to do that early in life from her mother.

Mae Belle's father was an unbeliever who emotionally and psychologically wounded all six of his children. Mae Belle was the firstborn, and she partnered with her godly mom in shepherding the other children. The stark contrast between her mother's Filter One kind of faith and her father's Filter Two mindset shaped her life. Her journey toward Filter One leadership began when she got a glimpse of the glory of God in Christ.

When she was nine, Mae Belle began to use "bad words" with her friends and to develop some sinful attitudes. She wanted to stay up past her bedtime, but her mother said she could only stay up if she watched Billy Graham on TV. Graham captivated her and made a statement that pierced her heart: "If you were the only person who ever lived, Jesus would still have died for you." She began to cry, repented of her sins, and placed her faith in Christ for salvation. The next day, her language changed, and her love for others began to grow. Seeing how Jesus treasured her moved her to treasure Him. I have had the joy of being her husband for forty-five years, and I have benefited immensely from her perseverance in trusting God.

One of the most dramatic Filter One leaders I have known didn't carry an official title, but her impact was undeniable. Aileen was an older single woman in our church who radically shaped the lives of a cluster of young handicapped men whom she "mothered" to maturity and faith in Christ.

When Aileen was in her late seventies, she desperately wanted to go on a tour of Israel that Mae Belle and I were preparing to lead. She urged me to pray that God would provide the funds for her to make this once-in-a-lifetime trip. After praying together for several weeks, she burst into my office and announced, "I have crashed my car, and I am going to Israel!" She explained that she had been in an accident in which no one was injured but her car was totaled. The payout from her insurance company was enough not only to purchase a good used car but also to pay for the trip! Aileen added, "I also had the joy of sharing the Gospel with the nice policeman who assisted me after the accident!"

Aileen had her faith filter in place!

So we all went to Israel together. When we reached Masada, we were making our way into the museum when Aileen suddenly ran back to the bus to get something she forgot. She missed two steps, flipped in the air, and broke her leg as she crashed on the hard pavement.

I rushed to her side, and as I bent toward her, she said, "Pastor Steve, I need my Gospel tracts off the bus so I can share Christ with people in the hospital." I told her there was no time for that and added, "Aileen *you* are the Gospel tract!" She was then rushed to the hospital in Beersheba.

As we continued our tour, I spoke with Aileen every day. She was almost giddy with joy! Her hospital roommate was a delightful Jewish woman, and their room was filled with the woman's family members each night. During the day and after the family left, Aileen and this young woman talked about the Bible. Aileen joyfully walked her through the entire story, answered her barrage of questions, and pointed her to Jesus Christ as the Messiah. The woman placed her faith in Jesus for salvation. They shared a few "overflowing with joy" days together before Aileen rejoined the team to head back to the USA.

Mae Belle and I, however, remained in Israel on a side tour for another few days. When we arrived home a week later, the church member who picked us up at the airport said, "We had Aileen's funeral yesterday. She died suddenly of complications from a blood clot."

When we passed the news on to her former roommate at Beersheba Hospital, the woman shared that Aileen told her, "I am thankful I broke my leg because it gave me the opportunity to meet you and introduce you to Jesus the Messiah."

HOW TO BE A FILTER ONE LEADER

If you are a follower of Christ, you know that you *should* filter life through the character and promises of God and not the other way around. After all, that is how we become Christians, by reversing our "faith filter" and turning from idols to serve the living God (1 Thessalonians 1:8–9). In addition, the only way to please God is to put our *faith* in His character and promises (Hebrews 11:6).

Jesus taught a pivotal insight which has helped me understand *how* to be a Filter One leader. It is built around his twice-repeated use of the word *must*.

*But He warned them and instructed them not to tell this to anyone, saying, "The Son of Man **must** suffer many things and be rejected by the elders and chief priests and scribes, and be killed and be raised up on the third day." And He was saying to them all, "If anyone wishes to come after Me, he **must** deny himself, and take up his cross daily and follow Me. For whoever wishes to save his life will lose it, but whoever loses his life for My sake, he is the one who will* *save it. For what is a man profited if he gains the whole world, and loses or forfeits himself?* (Luke 9:22–25)

Jesus's first *must* makes crystal clear He is determined to take the narrow road of death for us. This is His mission and the only way we can be rescued from our slavery to treasuring other gods. Jesus's *second must* is disturbing; *"If anyone wishes to come after Me, He **must** deny himself, take up his cross daily and follow Me."* According to Jesus, self-denial and death to self are essential if we are to be his disciples.

Jesus, a Jewish rabbi, used Hebrew parallelism to make his points. He makes a declaration and then follows it up with a parallel statement which clarifies the meaning of the first. First, He says, "You *must* deny yourself, take up your cross and follow Me." Then he clarifies, *"Whoever wishes to save his life will lose it and whoever loses his life for My sake will find it."*

The word for *life* that He used is significant. It is not the word for our physical life, *bios*, but our internal life, our *psyche*. In other words, He is referring to the treasure of our heart. What shapes our psyche? What do we look to for life, hope, and significance? What is the treasure of our heart? Jesus is saying, "If you want to follow Me, you must die to that treasure and shift your allegiance to Me. If you don't, you cannot be My disciple."

Now put the two *must* statements of Jesus together. Jesus always goes first. He said, *"I must* go and be killed and rise again." He does this because we are His treasure and He is willing to give everything to have us! Then He says, "If you want to be My disciple, *you must* deny yourself, take up your cross and follow Me." Jesus's *must* shapes our must! This is the *how* of it. When we see Him treasuring us, then we will treasure Him. Our greatest need is to see His glory, and when we do, we are compelled to trust Him. Seeing His glory compels us to filter our life through the character of God.

Isn't God good?

WORKOUTS TO THRIVE AND FINISH STRONG

Work through the following exercises and encourage a friend to join you. Stay at it until filtering life through the character and promises of God becomes second nature to you.

1. Review this chapter and share its basic concepts with someone else. Work through the following questions to ensure you understand the core truths:
   a. What foundational truth enabled Tom to cling to the goodness of God despite his circumstances?
   b. How does Jesus answer the ultimate *why* question, "What is the chief end of God?"
   c. How does Jesus provide us with the motivation we need to trust God?
   d. What reality must we embrace before we can fully trust God?
   e. How do the two "must statements" of Jesus go together? How do they teach us to trust God?
2. Memorize Scripture specifically targeted to reinforce your ability to see life through the lens of the character and promises of God. Some of my favorites are Romans 8:28–32, Romans 5:8, 1 John 4:10, Proverbs 3:5–6, Jeremiah 17:5–10, and Matthew 7:24–27.
3. Saturate your mind with the following key passages that will help you become a Filter One leader:
   a. Romans 8
   b. Galatians 3

    c. Hebrews 10

    d. John 10

    e. Jeremiah 15

    f. Matthew 7

    g. Isaiah 40

    h. Job 41

4. Study the following three famous conversions to Christ. What do they have in common? How do they differ? How did they each *obtain* a new way of viewing the world and how did they *strengthen* their "faith filter"?

    a. The Ethiopian   Acts 8:25–40

    b. Saul   Acts 9:1–31

    c. Cornelius   Acts 10:1–48

5. Contrast the two ways to live by examining the compelling story Jesus told in Luke 18:9–14. Describe the faith filter of each man. How are they alike? How do they differ? Why did Jesus declare one justified before God and the other not? On what basis?

6. Read Psalm 2 and contrast those who see God as a "royal pain" and those who see Him as a "blessed refuge."

CHAPTER 2

Be Shaped
by the Gospel

We proclaim Him, admonishing every man and teaching every man with all wisdom, so that we may present every man complete in Christ. For this purpose also I labor, striving according to His power, which mightily works within me.

—Colossians 1:28–29

As a leader, honestly ask yourself, "What is center stage in my life?" If your answer is not the good news of what God has done for you in Jesus Christ, then something else unworthy of your full allegiance has taken center stage in your life and ministry. *This puts you in danger.*

Only when you intentionally and consistently learn to be shaped by the Gospel of Jesus Christ will you be on the path of thriving and finishing strong.

If you do not let the Gospel constantly shape your thinking and behavior, you may help people, but you will not be connecting them to the power of God unto salvation. *This puts those under your influence in danger.*

God's answer to these twin dangers is to give you a passion to be shaped by the Gospel in every aspect of your life.

- The Holy Spirit, who permanently resides in you as a believer, is seeking to fuel this passion (Romans 8:1–17; Galatians 5:16–25; 2 Corinthians 3:18).
- Jesus Christ is calling you to embrace it fully (Luke 9:23–26).
- God the Father saved you for this purpose (Romans 8:28–29).
- The triune God is inviting you to join Him in His work of working out your salvation by being shaped by the Gospel (Philippians 2:12–13).

When the Gospel begins to shape your life, you will break through a thousand quitting points, have energy beyond yourself, be filled with hope, be infused with joy, be compelled to sacrificially love others, grow in discernment, and bring glory to God. It is what you were made for.

**Feed your passion to be shaped by the Gospel.
Delight in it.**

The prophets of the Old Testament strove to know what we have in the Gospel and the angels long to look at it (1 Peter 1:10–12). In Christ, we now have the full-diamond beauty of the Gospel, and looking at it transforms us (2 Corinthians 3:18). The Gospel is *not* just our entrance pass to salvation; it is

God's primary agent to mold and shape us into the image of Jesus Christ (Romans 1:16; Galatians 2:14). The Gospel breathes holy newness into every aspect of our lives: sexual ethics (1 Thessalonians 4:1–8), how we use our money (2 Corinthians 8:9), how we function at work (Colossians 3:23–25), how we relate to family members (Ephesians 5:22–6:3), parent our children (Ephesians 6:4, Colossians 3:21), use our time (Ephesians 5:16), view singleness (1 Corinthians 7:8–9, 17–20, 25–35), relate to the rich and poor (James 2:1–7), and face death (John 11:25–26). The list is almost endless!

The Gospel is the rock that Jesus Christ insisted we are to build our lives upon (Matthew 7:24–27). It alone has the power to radically change the affections of the human heart (Romans 1:16–17). It alone can make us humble and confident at the same time (Galatians 2:20). Its transforming power is remembered when we take communion or witness a baptism (Matthew 26:26–29; Matthew 28:18–20). It is relevant to every generation and every culture (1 Corinthians 9:19). As you daily read God's Word, ask Him to open your eyes to see, delight in, and be shaped by the Gospel.

**Grow your passion to be shaped by the Gospel.
Lead with it.**

In the last hour, I was again called to lead, and in the process, I was again shaped by the Gospel. Its truths gave me hope and provided perspective and comfort for a grieving family.

I just came from the bedside of a godly sixty-year-old man who has been the epitome of health. Two days ago, he was diagnosed with a very rare disease: Creutzfeldt-Jakob disease, a rare, degenerative, fatal brain disorder. Only one person in every million contracts the condition, but when it occurs—usually later in life—it tends to run its course very rapidly. My friend's doctors have given him a maximum of twelve months to live. In the time he has left, he will likely lose his eyesight, hearing, and the ability to walk.

Today, he was alert and upbeat, and his hope is clearly in Jesus Christ. As his family gathered around his bed, his godly twenty-four-year-old daughter asked me a question I have been asked a thousand times: "Why does God let things like this happen?"

I told her I would not give her a pat answer but share what has helped me the most through the years. I reminded her of the story line of the Bible: "God created everything good, the fall into sin corrupted everything, Jesus came to redeem us, and one day He will restore things to their good created order. So we live in a fallen world with disease and suffering, but we have a redeemer in Jesus and hope for full restoration in Him."

I then asked her, "How do you know God loves you?" She said, "I can feel it. The Holy Spirit lets me know." I said, "That is true, but the primary way we know God loves us is that Jesus died for us. We know love by this, not that we loved God but that He loved us and sent His Son to be the total satisfaction for our sins (1 John 4:10). Remember God has unlimited power, and bringing Jesus back from the dead for us demonstrates it. So measure God's power by the resurrection of Jesus, not your circumstances."

I asked her, "What is the only recorded question Jesus asked God the Father?" She immediately responded, "Why have you forsaken me?" I said, "Yes and that has helped me so many times to remember He understands what it is like to wonder why. In addition, the answer to *His* 'why' question is that God so loved us that He gave His only Son so that whoever believes in Him should not perish but have eternal life."

She said, "What you shared really helped."

We then anointed her dad with oil and prayed for his healing with the understanding that God is good and powerful and can heal—but even if He doesn't, God is still good and powerful (Daniel 3:16–18; James 5:13–16).

I was leading by letting the Gospel shape me and my response to people grappling with suffering. If I did not let the Gospel constantly shape my thinking and behavior, I might help people, but I would *not* be connecting them to the power of God unto salvation.

Leading with the Gospel empowers people and connects them to Jesus Christ. It means that I first let it shape me so that its truths guide the way I relate to others. Leading with the Gospel means we are constantly learning, praying, and seeking to grow in Christlikeness so that it shapes every aspect of our lives.

Mae Belle and I were greatly impressed by the humble leadership and Gospel-teachability of Josh Harris, the pastor made famous by his 1997 book *I Kissed Dating Goodbye* (Multnomah).[1] We watched his 2018 documentary, *I Survived "I Kissed Dating Goodbye."* In it, he shared his journey, some principles he taught that were out of alignment with the Gospel, and apologized for the negative impact his book had. He realized he had idealized marriage and misapplied the Gospel. His courage to admit his missteps was a courageous act that was itself rooted in his security in Christ.

In your leadership role, create a culture of leading with the Gospel. Talk about it often. Learn from those who are doing it well. Make it a core value, and multiply disciples who delight in and lead with it.

Expand your passion to be shaped by the Gospel. Connect with those who love it.

As a pastor for more than forty years, I have seen movements come and go through the evangelical world: Pentecostal-charismatic, biblical prophecy, spiritual gifts, the Moral Majority, body life, home churches, small groups, spiritual warfare, church growth, leadership, creationism, Christian family, unreached people groups, missional, social justice, racial reconciliation, emergence, megachurches, multi-site churches, and the Reformed and centrality of the Gospel movement.[2] These movements benefited the church in some ways and hindered it in others. However, of all the movements that have come along, the one that encourages me the most is the centrality of the Gospel movement.[3] I am referring to the biblical Gospel focused on the person and work of Jesus Christ on our behalf (1 Corinthians 15:1–10; Romans 1:16).

Make it a habit to connect with other leaders who are intentionally being shaped by the Gospel. Learn from each other, co-labor together, and help each other delight in it and lead with it.

Anticipate Gospel "Aha!" moments as you pray and persevere.

Not long ago, I was studying Acts 15 in preparation for a sermon. I knew the story well, and frankly, it seemed at first to be a dry, stale historical account of the first church council in history. Oh, joy! I was struggling with how the record of this gathering related to my life and our church family. I prayed and persevered.

Suddenly, the musty account sprang to life with relevant laser-beam insight. It was as if God was saying to me, "Don't you get it? This is the golden key for yourself and the church family you pastor to flourish generation after generation after generation! Pay attention!" I literally shouted, "Wow! I have never seen it quite so *clearly* before!" You had one excited preacher in his study!

I hope you will stick with me as we walk through this extremely relevant passage of Scripture. We will linger because the insights are so life-giving and reveal a core essential for ministry leaders to thrive and finish strong.

THE DESTINY-SHAPING CONTEXT OF ACTS 15

Acts 15 is placed in the middle of two of the most effective advancements of the Gospel of Jesus Christ in history: Paul's first and second missionary adventures, which transformed the culture of the Mediterranean world and launched a global movement which continues today. Then abruptly, this rapid movement of the Gospel was threatened by an enemy from within. If left unchecked, it would have divided, sidelined, and suffocated the church. Acts 15 tells us how the church faced this threat, defeated it, and moved ahead in unity. *This is vital information for us today!*

Acts 15 records a destiny-shaping decision of the early church and is both a warning and call to action for us.

First, it alerts us to *the* danger *every* believer and *every* church faces in every generation. And it's a threat so powerful that, if not countered, it will turn us away from the heart of God's message to the world.

Second, it teaches us in story form (one of the best ways to learn) the *only way* to stand firm against the looming threat so we can move ahead in unity.

The scourge surfaced after Paul and Barnabas returned from their first missionary journey to Antioch, Syria (Acts 14:24–28). Some teachers who claimed to be representing the Jerusalem church sought to plant an idea that would have sucked the life out of it. Acts 15:1–5 tells the story:

Some men came down from Judea and began teaching the brethren, **"Unless you are circumcised according to the custom of Moses, you cannot be saved."** *And when Paul and Barnabas had great dissension and debate with them, the brethren determined that Paul and Barnabas and some others of them should go up to Jerusalem to the apostles and elders concerning this issue. Therefore, being sent on their way by the church, they were passing through both Phoenicia and Samaria, describing in detail the conversion of the Gentiles, and were bringing great joy to all the brethren. When they arrived at Jerusalem, they were received by the church and the apostles and the elders, and they reported all that God had done with them. But some of the sect of the Pharisees who had believed stood up, saying,* **"It is necessary to circumcise them and to direct them to observe the Law of Moses."** (Emphasis mine.)

A JESUS-PLUS APPROACH TO SALVATION

The Pharisees insisted that the Gentiles who had placed their faith in Jesus Christ for salvation also needed to be circumcised to be saved. This was like arsenic in the water of salvation! They were declaring that faith in Jesus Christ was not enough. They were preaching a "Jesus-plus" salvation. Paul and Barnabas had an intense debate with them, and the church wisely decided to send the team to Jerusalem to settle the matter once and for all.

The mistake these Pharisees made is the same mistake many of us make. They denied the Gospel by adding to it.

First, they missed a pattern God had clearly revealed in Genesis 15 regarding Abraham. Long before Abraham was circumcised, he was declared righteous before God by faith: *"Then he (Abraham) believed the Lord; and it was reckoned to him as righteousness"* (Genesis 15:6). Circumcision was a *sign* of the covenant (Genesis 17:9–11) not a *source* of salvation (Galatians 5:2).

Second, they missed the purpose of the Law. The Law was not given as a means of earning our salvation but to convince us of our sin and our need for a savior (Romans 3:20; James 2:10). The law reveals God's holiness, exposes our sin, and points us to the only One who fulfilled its demands in our place: Jesus Christ (Galatians 3:13–14).

Many believe it was around this time that Paul wrote the book of Galatians, in which he makes crystal clear that a gospel which adds anything to the work of Christ as necessary for salvation is false. His language is absolute: You are accursed if you embrace any other gospel than the one you have received from the apostles of Christ (Galatians 1:6–9).

- The moment you insist on a Jesus-plus approach to salvation, you *dethrone* Jesus and *devalue* His death for our sins and His resurrection from the dead (Galatians 2:21).
- The moment you embrace a Jesus-plus approach to salvation, you lose your assurance of salvation and no longer have a good-news gospel (Galatians 3:1–9).
- A Jesus-plus approach to salvation is arrogant and demonically destructive because it reverses the divine order of salvation (Galatians 2:16)—acceptance by

grace through faith *followed* by obedience (Ephesians
2:8–10; Galatians 2:20; 5:13–24).

The "Jesus-plus" non-gospel is this: "I must obey or add
something to the work of Jesus; *then* I will be accepted before
God." The default mode of the human heart is a works-
based, Jesus-plus approach to salvation. This is *the* great danger we face in our walk with God. This danger is both subtle
and persistent.

I have personally tasted the misery of this Jesus-plus gospel
and have engaged with thousands over the years who have been
devastated by it. The inevitable result of adding *anything* to the
work of Christ for our salvation is deceptive pride and self-
righteousness (thinking we could add to His finished work) or
despair (thinking we could never be or do enough to obtain
salvation). Pride and despair are *not* fruits of the Gospel but the
symptoms of the disease of a Jesus-plus approach to salvation.

During college, I had an encounter with an intoxicated
fraternity brother who exposed my *pride*, the "surface life" I was
living, and pushed me to *despair*.

John was intoxicated and left the party at two in the morning. He was working his way up the steps to his room in the
fraternity house when he spotted me. I was at my post on the
stairs that weekend, waiting to help the next intoxicated brother
get safely to his bed.

As the teetotaler chaplain of the house, I was doing my best
to live for Christ and care for my fraternity brothers, yet I carried
around an emptiness that haunted me. My relationship with
God frustrated me. I sincerely loved Jesus Christ but lacked
power, purpose, and peace in my life. I correctly understood that
Jesus died for my sins and rose from the dead so that I could
have eternal life. However, *what I believed about how this works*

out in daily life became a trap. I believed coming to Christ was like buying fire insurance and signing up for a self-improvement program! Jesus would keep me out of Hell, and I was to keep myself out of sin. I thought my job was to repeatedly rededicate myself to trying harder and doing all I could to *earn God's approval.* My perspective confined me to a rigid external morality that puffed me up when I "kept the rules" and heaped guilt on me when I failed. My focus on trying to be good enough to please God fed my deep sense of insecurity and pride. In this context, my attempts at sharing Christ with my fraternity brothers were always greeted with a polite "No, thank you."

My inebriated fraternity brother sat down beside me, looked me in the eye, and shattered my world with a short message. "King, you are the most miserable man in this house. I hope you find what you are looking for."

He walked away and left me devastated in the darkness. Questions with no answers raced through my mind: "What is missing in my life?" "Why does God seem so far away?" "How do I climb out of this hole of misery?" His words exposed my sincere, yet crippled, relationship with God and sent me on a quest to find stability, significance, and purpose in life. I needed change below the surface at the heart level.

A few weeks after my fraternity brother declared me miserable, I went home for the summer. I longed to find the hope my friend had wished for me. My brother Andy immediately captured my attention. His life had changed. He joyfully spoke of Jesus Christ and engaged with the Bible and its truths in a way that gave him purpose, peace, and love. His girlfriend and her father had shared some basic truths about walking with Christ that had a profound impact on his life. I gleaned all I could from Andy, went to church with him, and rededicated my life to Christ.

After the morning worship service, a group of men in the church approached me. They told me they had been praying for me while I was away at college. They invited me to attend a two-week leadership training institute sponsored by Campus Crusade for Christ (now Cru), which was being held in California for college students from across the nation. They had agreed to cover all expenses, and I gladly accepted their offer.

The two weeks at Arrowhead Springs, Crusade's headquarters, transformed my life. I learned core essentials of how to enjoy my relationship with Christ—my identity in Christ, how to walk in the power of the Holy Spirit, how to share my faith, how to know God's will, how to study the Bible, and more. I learned how to apply the Gospel and its truths to my heart; as a result, my attitude and behavior began to change.

We were trained to share our faith and spent a day engaging with people on the beaches. My partner and I approached a group of men sitting around a campfire and asked if we could share with them. To my astonishment, they eagerly listened as we walked through the Gospel presentation. Then each man prayed to receive Christ! Later that day, we returned to Arrowhead Springs and hundreds of students shared amazing stories of people placing their faith in Christ through their witness.

Something went off inside me, and my heart was captured. That night, I sat in the dark overlooking San Bernardino and thanked God for answering my fraternity brother's concern for me. I did find what I was looking for! As I gazed at the lights scattered across the darkness, I sensed God telling me, "This is My plan for you, to share the Gospel and spread My light in the darkness."

In the fall, I returned to college, resigned as chaplain of the fraternity, and became the vice president instead. Over the next two years, more than twenty of my fraternity brothers placed their faith in Christ, and after graduation, six of us went into the ministry. The radical change in my life and many of my fraternity brothers' lives was directly tied to the foundational truths we learned about how to know Jesus Christ and walk with Him. I had discovered how to move from moralism and behavior modification to applying the Gospel to my heart!

STAND FIRM: CONTEND FOR THE GOSPEL AND KEEP IT CENTRAL

As we continue through Acts 15, we will discover why the Gospel must be central, and we will equip you with two tools that will help you and those you lead move from "living on the surface" to experiencing change from the heart.[4]

Do you find yourself swinging like a pendulum between pride over your progress to despair over your failures? Do you often compare yourself with others and feel superior or inferior? We will discover how to escape that ugly cycle and replace it with lasting change from a heart-gospel interchange.[5]

Acts 15:6–21 tells us Peter, Paul, Barnabas, James (the half-brother of Jesus), and representatives of the Jewish and Gentile churches *all* rejected a Jesus-plus approach to salvation. They affirmed the gospel of salvation by grace alone through faith alone in Christ alone.[6]

*After there had been much debate, Peter stood up and said to them, "Brethren, you know that in the early days God made a choice among you, that by my mouth the Gentiles would hear the word of the gospel and believe. And God, who knows the heart, testified to them giving them the Holy Spirit, just as He also did to us; and He made no distinction between us and them, cleansing their hearts by faith. Now therefore why do you put God to the test by placing upon the neck of the disciples **a yoke** which neither our fathers nor we have* *been able to bear? But we believe that we are saved through the grace of the Lord Jesus, in the same way as they also are."* (Acts 15:7–11, emphasis mine)

Notice he calls the Law "a yoke which neither our fathers nor we have been able to bear." The Law, given to Moses from God, revealed God's holy character and clarified how the people of God were to live as His distinct people. However, no one could fulfill the Law perfectly. Therefore, God made provision for their sin through the temple sacrifices and priesthood. Jesus Christ, the Messiah, fulfilled the demands of the Law *for us* as the true temple of God, the ultimate High Priest, and the final sacrifice for our sins (Hebrews 8–10). Peter is crystal clear: "We believe that we (Jews) are saved through the grace of the Lord Jesus, in the same way as they (Gentiles) also are" (Acts 15:11).

Next, Barnabas and Paul speak and provide an overview of their missionary journey and how God worked to draw many Gentiles to faith in Christ (Acts 15:12; 13–14). Those assembled rejoiced over hearing of the Gentiles coming to faith in Christ (Acts 15:4). *None* of the Gentiles had been required to be circumcised to be saved.

Acts 15:13–19 tells us: "After they had stopped speaking, James answered, saying, "Brethren, listen to me. Simeon has related how *God first concerned Himself about taking from among the Gentiles a people for His name.* With this the words of the Prophets agree . . . Therefore, it is my judgment that *we do not trouble those who are turning to God from among the Gentiles . . .*"

Acts 15:13–19 tells us: "After they had stopped speaking, James answered, saying, "Brethren, listen to me. Simeon has related how *God first concerned Himself about taking from among the Gentiles a people for His name.* With this the words of the Prophets agree . . . Therefore, it is my judgment that *we do not trouble those who are turning to God from among the Gentiles . . ."*

James says, "You have heard from Peter how God has taken from the Gentiles a people for His name, as the Old Testament prophets said would happen." He uses the words of the prophet Amos to say what he believed all the prophets taught to one degree or another. *Therefore, Peter, Paul, Barnabas, and James all agree the Gentiles are saved by grace alone through faith alone in Christ alone. They reject a Jesus-plus approach to salvation.*

James then states his judgment in Acts 15:19: "Therefore . . . do not trouble those who are turning to God from among the Gentiles." How would they trouble the Gentiles? They would trouble them by telling them, "You have not done enough by trusting Jesus alone for salvation." Paul referred to this kind of Gospel-denying trouble in his letter to the Galatians (Galatians 1:7–9; 3:1; 5:2–3, 8–10; 6:11–13).

However, what James said next may trouble *you!* He said, "But that we write to them that they abstain from things contaminated by idols and from fornication and from what is strangled and from blood" (Acts 15:20). James grounded these prohibitions in a cultural context; these Gentile believers were in ongoing relationship with Jewish believers who have been shaped by the law of Moses: "For Moses from ancient generations has in every city those who preach him, since he is read in the synagogues every Sabbath." (Acts 15:21).

The restrictions on the Gentile believers were not a *requirement for* salvation but an *expression of* their salvation. Because they are now one in Christ with the Jewish believers, they should allow the Gospel to change their behavior and relationships with those from a different background. Their unity and ongoing growth in Christ are to be maintained by applying the

Gospel and its truths to every aspect of their lives. The Gentile believers came from a culture of sexual and dietary permissiveness and could therefore easily offend their Jewish brothers and sisters in Christ. James is calling these Gentile believers in Christ to let the Gospel transform their sexual morality and relationships with their Jewish brethren.

This new, racially diverse church had *one* hope of unity— the functional centrality of the Gospel.

All who were *saved* by believing the Gospel are now to live in unity by being constantly *shaped by* the Gospel. The truth of salvation by faith alone in Christ alone as taught by the Scriptures alone was the rallying point of unity and the key to the unhindered advancement of the Gospel from generation to generation.

- *Only* when we allow the Gospel to shape every aspect of our lives can we experience unity among racially diverse peoples.
- *Only* when the Gospel is central do we give the Triune God—Father, Son, and Holy Spirit— proper honor.
- *Only* when the Gospel is at the core of our lives and gathered community do we escape the straitjacket of legalism and the pit of license.

The Jerusalem Council composed a letter to the Gentile believers in Christ and sent it to them with Paul, Barnabas, and a delegation representing the council (Acts 15:28–29). The message was clear: Gentile believers did *not* need to be circumcised to be saved. Faith in Jesus Christ is the *one* requirement for all to have salvation (Acts 4:12).

The council's conclusion and letter affirmed their unity in Christ with Gentile believers and their adherence to salvation by grace alone through faith alone in Christ alone. It also urged Gentile believers to be directed by the Gospel demands of sexual purity and loving sensitivity to those of diverse backgrounds. The letter was joyfully received, and the church continued to be strengthened (Acts 15:30–35). Their contention for the Gospel and resulting unity around it diverted the danger and enabled the church to flourish! Their unity was built around the Gospel functioning in their leadership and daily lives.

We must learn how to let the Gospel and its truths breathe life into every aspect of our existence. This is especially true when we study, teach, and preach the Bible. If we don't develop this skill, we will end up teaching moral lessons and willpower-based behavior modification, not Gospel transformation!

When the Gospel is central, our preaching moves from moral lessons to ongoing transformation.

Every four years, our church selects a people group that has not been exposed to the Gospel on which to focus our prayers and resources with the goal of establishing a multiplying, Gospel-centered church among them. In 2014, we selected the Kalal people of India because our research indicated no known believers among them. We partnered with a team from East-West Mission, which had planted over a thousand house churches among similar people groups. We sponsored five church planters and sent teams in to assist them. After four years, there are now more than three hundred house churches and a growing movement of the Gospel!

Now we are training the new pastors of these house churches. Recently, I was part of a team equipping them to preach Gospel-centered sermons. We noted a tendency among the trainees to turn Bible messages into moral lessons built on self-effort instead of faith in the Gospel.

They needed to learn to preach Christ every time, which alone shows how the whole Bible fits together. Instead of beginning their training with a passage and showing them how to turn it into a Gospel-centered message, we *began* by giving them what most believers miss—the story line of the Bible, which demonstrates *why* the Gospel of Jesus Christ is its central message. Once this framework was clearly in their minds, learning how to develop a Gospel-centered message from any text came naturally.[7] We taught them that every time you expound a Bible text, you must show how we cannot save ourselves and only Jesus can. In addition, we stressed that being in Christ gives us a new identity and power which changes our lives. And suddenly, their sermons took on new power. Every Bible lesson and story pointed to Jesus and how He can change us at the heart level.

One of the pastors shared how he saw the story of David and Goliath in a new way. It was not just about us mustering up the faith to slay our giants. Instead, it pointed to One greater than David, Jesus Christ, Who destroyed our greatest enemy, sin. We, like the army of Israel, have courage because of what He did for us. He was beginning to understand that preaching a message from the Bible without pointing to the overall story of Jesus would just be a "try harder" message instead of a "faith in the work of Christ" message. All the pastors were excited to discover that every ethical and moral command given to believers in Jesus is rooted in and based on our union with Christ, which we express by the power of the Holy Spirit.[8]

These Gospel-centered messengers have now seen whole communities transformed. They are providing health clinics, job training, sports programs, and marriage and family training—all with a Gospel-centered focus.

If you remove this intentional focus on the centrality of the Gospel, Christianity will come across as just another self-improvement process aimed at only reforming our behavior. Only when we intentionally keep the Gospel central can we communicate that Christianity is about obtaining a new identity in Christ and living in the power of the Holy Spirit for the glory of God.[9]

When the Gospel is central, we can safely explore difficult issues and work out solutions together.

Racism and justice are directly related to the Gospel, yet exploring these issues can spark conflict and prick emotional wounds. Our elders are taking a year to read two Gospel-centered books on these issues and learn to listen to each other and our diverse church family. Our unity around the Gospel and determination to keep it central has made the process more helpful than hurtful.[10]

We have a diverse church family with people from multiple religious, social, and political backgrounds. Before joining, we require people to go through a membership class to learn our mission, core values, doctrines, and approach to ministry, and that class is followed by an interview with an elder. Central to all of this is the Gospel. We make sure we all understand and believe the Gospel and learn how to apply its core truths to every area of our lives. Doing so has fostered unity in our church family, which celebrates our diversity at the same time.

TWO TOOLS TO BE SHAPED BY THE GOSPEL

Learning how to be shaped by the Gospel is an *essential* which will enable us to flourish and finish strong. We have developed two tools and put them to use in our own life and ministry. They have been a tremendous help to me and hundreds of others. I use both tools every day and have found them to be extremely helpful in keeping me Gospel-centered. We call them The Gospel U and The Four-Fold Praise. You can find them in the appendix.

Learning to look beneath our life issues and examine our hearts is a learned skill which the Holy Spirit prompts us to develop. One of the Holy Spirit's functions is to convict us of sin and to point us to Jesus Christ (John 16:8–11, 14).

For example, one of my heart issues is tied to control, and when it is threatened, I can become angry. When I sense a lack of control over issues that are my responsibility, I can become emotionally intense and express myself in anger.

Recently, I was in a staff meeting with the team I love and who love me. We were evaluating our worship services, as we do every week, when someone commented on an announcement I had made regarding a ministry I considered important. I felt unsupported by the team and unjustly criticized. Instead of calmly expressing my concerns and asking questions to clarify the issue, I reacted in anger and refused to listen to any other perspective but my own. The team graciously tried to give me a broader perspective, but I was locked in the prison of my own self-centeredness and could not hear them.

I went home to my study and prayed. I replayed the criticism and began to justify my anger. But then, while I prayed, I sensed the conviction of the Holy Spirit. I noticed the bright red cover of a book on my stack of "need to read" books. The big black and white words of its title immediately grabbed my attention: *Good and Angry: Redeeming Anger, Irritation, Complaining and Bitterness* by David Powlison (New Growth Press, 2016). That book should have had my picture on the front!

I sat down and began to read the book. I was captured by the author's insights on two kinds of anger. He called "bad anger" selfish and destructive. He described "good anger" as being concerned with the welfare of others and expressed in *constructive* displeasure.

When the author began to unpack what bad anger looks like, I read a sentence that showed me how far from the Gospel my heart had drifted. The sentence that slapped me awake said, "Our bad anger shouts out, 'My kingdom come! My will be done! Judgment and wrath upon all who transgress against me!'"

I had to face the truth: No one *made* me mad. My anger was not someone else's fault. I had to take responsibility for my bad anger, and I had to repent. I faced the fact that I had looked to my self-justification as a "savior" and had treated the living Christ as a corpse. When I saw the truth and admitted it to God, I was turning back to the Gospel of the living Christ. He has called me to lose my life in Him to find it. I had not valued the opinion of the team and was unwilling to listen to perspectives that did not agree with mine. I did not respond to the negative comment with humility and did not seek to learn from it. Jesus Christ was not on the throne of my life in that instant, and I did not look to Him to empower me to act in wisdom.

I went back to the team, took responsibility for my sin, and asked their forgiveness. I explained what I had learned about anger and how the Holy Spirit had convicted me and pointed me to Christ. My behavior changed because a heart-gospel interchange had taken place. The team graciously forgave me, and we had a healthy discussion on how to respond to feedback with wisdom. I was learning and modeling how to be shaped by the Gospel. And you need to make this a priority in your own life.

WHAT IS CENTER STAGE IN YOUR LIFE?

I am well acquainted with the writings of an internationally known Gospel-centered leader. He has thirteen bestsellers to his name, and his proven skills at cross-cultural missions and disciple-making launched a movement that has gone global for generations. He suffered for the Gospel; he was falsely accused and languished in prison for years. He lost his good health, many of his friends forsook him, some of the churches he planted were overrun by false teachers because the church family believed lies they told about him, and his financial support dried up. Yet he never lost hope. Amazingly, in that context he wrote a book on joy!

The apostle Paul was constantly shaped by the Gospel, and as a result, he had a purpose that no amount of suffering and confinement could take from him. It is obvious to any who read his bestsellers what was center stage in his life—Jesus Christ. As a Gospel-shaped leader, he escaped the double dangers we opened this chapter with—the danger of allegiance to a cheap "Jesus substitute" and the danger of influencing others away from Christ.

I close with his inspired words and pray that you, along with me, will fully surrender to the same Lord he followed.

We proclaim Him, admonishing every man and teaching every man with all wisdom, so that we may present every man complete in Christ. For this purpose also I labor, striving according to His power, which mightily works within me.

—Colossians 1:28–29

Workouts to Thrive and Finish Strong

Learning to apply the Gospel to all the issues of our life is a skill Jesus Christ is eager to help us learn. He has given us the Word of God, the Spirit of God, and the people of God to assist us. To hone your skills at responding to life with a *heart-gospel interchange*, work through the following exercises.

1. The Corinthian church was one of the most dysfunctional in the New Testament. Divisions, sexual immorality, lawsuits, weak marriages, selfishness, misuse of spiritual gifts, denial of core doctrines, and pride were all issues that needed to be confronted with the Gospel. Read 1 Corinthians 1:1–17 and answer the following questions.
   a. How did Paul *begin* his confrontation of the church (1:1–9)?
   b. What did he remind them of *before* he appealed for a change in their behavior? Why?
   c. What Gospel truths did he anchor his exhortations to them in? (1 Corinthians 1:10–17).
2. In each of the following passages, identify the change in behavior that is called for and the basis of the exhortation to change. Identify the "heart-Gospel" interchange that is called for before a change in behavior can occur.

	Heart-Gospel Interchange	Behavior Change
Romans 6		
Romans 12		
1 Corinthians 10		
Galatians 5–6		
Ephesians 4–6		
Colossians 3–4		

CHAPTER 3

Align Your Life

What is it that Jesus Christ died for, lives in, works through, prays for, is perfecting, is coming back for, and will spend eternity delighting in?

Sir Percival Lowell was a famous nineteenth-century astronomer who founded Lowell Observatory in Flagstaff, Arizona. He was fixated on Mars and was convinced that an intelligent civilization once flourished there. His idea was based on an intricate set of canals he observed through his telescope. He drew diagrams of them, published articles and books supporting his theory—and because he was so respected, many believed him.[1]

More than a century later, space probes and rovers have explored Mars, and the planet has been extensively mapped and studied—but no canals have been found. What was Lowell looking at? We now know that he had a rare eye disease, one that some have called Lowell's syndrome. He was tracing the veins of his own eyeballs! Percival Lowell was sincere in his beliefs and diligent in his observations, but it turned out he was out of touch with reality when it came to Mars.

Ministry leaders can develop spiritual Lowell's syndrome, too: We become so busy tracing the veins of our own circumstances and reinforcing our assumptions that we simply cannot accept another view of reality. We can end up out of alignment with God's purposes and lead ministries built on our assumptions.

But ministry leaders who intentionally align their lives *with what Jesus is building* are on the path to thriving and finishing strong!

Don't *assume* you know what Jesus is building. I did that for years, and ended up dishonoring what Jesus cherishes without even realizing I was out of alignment with His primary purposes. I will share that confession with you at the end of this chapter.

Jesus is fulfilling His redemptive and restorative purposes through people, and His sovereign rule means that He accomplishes His purposes through both those who belong to Him *and those who do not* (John 19:11; Acts 2:23; Luke 19:10; Matthew 28:18–20).[2]

However, Jesus is *directly* working through His people as they fulfill their unique callings (Ephesians 2:10; Colossians 3:23; 1 Corinthians 10:31).[3] As the Reformers taught, all legitimate callings are sacred, and God works through all His people to accomplish His purposes.

Since this book is aimed specifically at ministry leaders, I will be focusing on God's work through His church. As all believers are part of the body of Christ, we will focus specifically on Jesus's promise that He would build His church (1 Corinthians 12:13; Matthew 16:18).

If I ask what Jesus is building, you may immediately answer, "He is building His church!" But do you know what *Jesus said*

His church is? Can you clearly define, *from Scripture*, its essential traits? Do those who follow you *understand biblically* what a church is and why it is so important to Jesus?

If you are in the least bit vague in your response to *any* of those questions, then this chapter is going to encourage and equip you and those you lead. If you do not have clear biblically based answers to these questions, it may indicate misalignment with God's purposes and evidence of spiritual Lowell's syndrome.

EXAMINE YOUR ASSUMPTIONS

Church is a hot issue today among young, entrepreneurial pastors. As a result, there are countless innovative church plants across the nation. Many books regarding how to function effectively as a church have been published. I have read dozens of them and benefited from their insights. Their titles always end with the word "church"—*Simple Church, Just Church, Everyday Church, Purpose-Driven Church, Emerging Church, Missional Church, Total Church, Multi-Site Church, Ancient-Future Church,* and many others. The irony is that almost none of the books define what a church is—the definition is *assumed.* Most of the books share effective practices gleaned from other "successful" churches. But without a clear, biblically based definition of what a church is, how do you determine if it is successful or not? It is dangerous to build churches on an *assumed* definition!

I recently conducted a survey over a period of several weeks in which I asked people to define what a church is. I asked pastors, missionaries, ministry leaders, church members, neighbors, business leaders, and unbelievers. Answers ranged from blank stares or a list of certain aspects of what churches do to statements that are found nowhere in the Bible. *No one* gave me a clear definition of what a church is. Too often, we live by assumptions or traditions which have been passed down to us. When we attempt to define what a church is, we struggle to be specific.

I have served on a mission board for nearly thirty years and seen it grow from a small operation headquartered in the founder's basement to a global network of more than twenty sending bases. Its mission is to launch *church-planting movements* among those who have never heard of Jesus Christ. Several years ago, when we were reviewing our core documents and mission statement, it dawned on us that nowhere in our documents did we define what a church is—yet our mission is to plant churches! We had simply assumed the definition! We determined to correct the oversight. We commissioned a team to study what the New Testament teaches regarding the church and define its core characteristics. The resulting clarity has been extremely helpful!

According to the Bible, a church is not a building, denomination, Bible study, small group, online community, outreach team, preaching center, worship gathering, activity center, social service agency, seminary, or missions agency. A church may be engaged in many of these activities and gather in one place, but none of them alone define a church.

Fortunately, God has not left us in the dark regarding what Jesus is building. He has clearly revealed in the New Testament the essential definition of Christ's church, both locally and globally.

Our task as ministry leaders is to know this essential biblical definition and use it as a grid to align our lives and those we lead with God's purposes. We are to do this humbly, as those who have lived on assumptions, and yet confidently, as those who are now anchored in God's revelation in Scripture. Let's turn our back on *assuming* what a church is. Let's refuse to settle for vague concepts about it. Lowell's syndrome no more!

Intentionally aligning our lives with what Jesus is doing in and through His church is an essential for leaders who long to thrive and finish strong.

Many do not believe the bolded statement you just read. Go back and read it again.

Christian leaders, including me, may form our ideas about the church more from culture and tradition than Scripture. This is no light issue because the Scriptures tell us that Jesus bought His church with His blood, works through her, constantly prays for her, is perfecting her as His bride, is coming back for her, and will spend eternity delighting in her. We are stepping onto holy ground and dealing with what God says is sacred—His church.

Contrast the way Jesus regards His bride with the way we consider her. We often do not treat her as sacred. At worst, we treat her as disposable and out of date. We also often move in judgment and criticism, making it all about us and our agenda. We easily foster a "whatever works" mindset and ignore God's clear directives for what He calls sacred.

So let's explore the sacred texts of Scripture and then purpose to align our lives and those we lead with the church Jesus is building.

The Greek word translated "church," *ekklesia,* is sprinkled through the New Testament 114 times. It consists of *ek,* meaning "out of," and *klesia,* meaning "to call." The church is *people* who have been "called out" by God and have placed their faith in Jesus Christ for salvation. Many metaphors are used to describe Jesus's church, such as body, bride, flock, building, priest, and family. Jesus bought the church with His blood (Acts 20:28; 1 Corinthians 6:19–20). He ever lives to make intercession for her (Hebrews 7:25) and considers persecution of His church to be persecution of Himself (Acts 9:4).

Let's discover the core essentials of the church by consulting the three best sources: Jesus, the founder and head of the church; Paul, the greatest missionary of the church; and Doctor Luke, her first historian. There are many other biblical references and resources I will recommend, but these three will root us in the core essentials of what a church is.

WHAT DID JESUS SAY ABOUT HIS CHURCH?

Jesus described His church in many ways; however, the New Testament only records Him using the term *ekklesia* twice. In Matthew 16:18, where Jesus says, "I will build My church," He refers to what theologians have called the universal or invisible church. It is made up of all believers in Christ in every generation both in Heaven and on earth. It is called "universal" because it includes all believers in Christ and "invisible" because it consists of believers both in Heaven and on earth (Ephesians 1:13–14; Revelation 5:8–13; 19:7–10). In Matthew 18:15–17, Jesus tells us to bring unrepentant believers, after a first and second warning, to the church. Here, Jesus refers to the local church, gathered in a specific place. Therefore, Jesus's church is both universal and local.

It is interesting that of the 114 times the New Testament uses the word "church," ninety refer to the local church and the rest to the universal or global church. Therefore, the primary focus in the New Testament is on the local church, though it does not neglect its global identity.

Jesus intentionally used a shocking setting to speak with His disciples about His church. He brought them into the region of Caesarea Philippi (Matthew 16:13).

My wife and I have had the joy of leading several tours to Israel. One of my favorite places is Caesarea Philippi. It is in northern Israel, near the ancient city of Dan, and it is home to many springs which eventually form the Jordan River. In Jesus's day, Caesarea Philippi was a vibrant city. It derived its name from Philip, son of Herod the Great and Caesar Augustus, whom Philip named the city after. In Jesus's day, no rabbi would dare take his disciples to this region. It was like Las Vegas on triple steroids! It contained several pagan temples built in front of a large rock quarry dedicated to the worship of Pan and other gods. Images of these deities were displayed in rock niches, and sacred fertility rites took place in the temples. A giant spring gushing from a cave just behind one of the temples was called *The Gates of Hades.* It was believed that the gods would descend during the winter into the seemingly bottomless pool of water in the cave and rise again in the spring. Sacrifices, sexual acts, and rituals were performed to win the favor of the fertility gods.

Jesus took His disciples into this pagan environment and began to question them about how people perceived His identity.

Now when Jesus came into the district of Caesarea Philippi, He was asking His disciples, "Who do people say that the Son of Man is?" And they said, "Some say John the Baptist; and others, Elijah; but still others, Jeremiah, or one of the prophets." He said to them, "But who do you say that I am?" Simon Peter answered, "You are the Christ, the Son of the living God." And Jesus said to him, "Blessed are you, Simon Barjona, because flesh and blood did not reveal this to you, but My Father who is in heaven" (Matthew 16:13–17).

Jesus declared Peter blessed because his understanding of Jesus's identity as the Christ, the Son of the *living* God, was revealed to Him by God the Father. This revelation was in stark contrast to the *dead* gods in the rocks before them.

Jesus then made a specific statement about His church and related it to Peter and the surrounding pagan environment they were standing in: *"I also say to you that you are Peter, and upon this rock I will build My church; and the gates of Hades will not overpower it"* (Matthew 16:18*)*. The Greek word Jesus used for Peter is *petros*, which means "a stone." The Greek word Jesus used for rock is *petra*, which means "large rock, quarry, or bedrock." The disciples were observing the large bedrock wall on which the pagan gods were being worshiped. Jesus told Peter, "You are *a stone* and upon *this bedrock*, I will build My church."

Obviously, Peter, a stone, and bedrock are not the same thing. Some believe the bedrock refers to Peter's confession of Christ as the Son of God (Matthew 16:16). Others believe the bedrock is a reference to the band of disciples because Paul says in Ephesians 2:20 that "the *church was built upon the foundation of the apostles and prophets."* Others believe Jesus is saying, "I will build My church upon this bedrock of paganism and overcome it." Regardless of the view one takes, what is clear is that the church belongs to Jesus Christ and He is the One who is building it.

It is fascinating to place Jesus's promise that *"the gates of Hades* will not overpower it" in the context of the setting in which He said it—in front of the spring called by that name. Gates are a place of defense, and the ruins of the walled city near this worship site make that very clear. Jesus is saying that His church is an invading force, fulfilling His redemptive and restorative purposes, and one that will chase Hell back to its gates!

To the outside observer at Caesarea Philippi, Jesus and His band of disciples must have seemed insignificant and powerless compared to the power of Rome and its gods. Today, that city, the rock of the gods, and the gates of Hades are a pile of rubble. The hosts of gods once worshiped there are largely unknown, except to tour guides and archaeologists. On the other hand, *Jesus's church is a vast global family which is chasing Hell back to its*

*gates and fulfilling His redemptive and restorative purposes genera-
tion after generation!*

The keys which open the door to the Kingdom of Heaven
are given to those who believe Jesus is the Christ, the Son of the
living God (Matthew 16:19). When the Gospel of Christ is
preached and believed, people are ushered into the kingdom
(Colossians 1:13–14; Luke 23:42–43; John 3:3; 2 Timothy 4:18).

Wow! Jesus is chasing Hell back to its gates *through* His
church! He has given *us* the Gospel keys that open the door to
the Kingdom of Heaven! He is building His church *through* His
church. Dare we, as ministry leaders, consider His church
optional and out of date?

JESUS ALWAYS COMES WITH HIS FAMILY!

Jesus never intended to have those who join His mission "go it
alone." He and the Father sent us the Holy Spirit (John 14:16),
and He promised to never leave us (Matthew 28:20).

Being united to Jesus Christ *includes* being united to His
family (1 Corinthians 1:13; 12:1–31). Can you imagine becoming close friends with a man by telling him, "You know, I really
want a relationship with you, but I don't like your wife"? In our
individualistic culture, we often develop a "Jesus and *me* mindset" and ignore the fact that He wants us to have a "Jesus and
we" mindset.

Being in alignment with Jesus and His purposes includes
a threefold connection: obedience to the *Word of God*, submission to the *Spirit of God*, and intentional connection with the
people of God (Ephesians 5:15–21; Colossians 3:16–17).

Did you know there are twenty-eight "one-another" commands in the New Testament? We are to love one another,
encourage one another, pray for one another, bear one another's

burdens, and more. It is *impossible* to fulfill these commands without a commitment to a local group of believers.

Have you bought the lie that faithfulness to Jesus and devotion to His family can be separated? For example, do you agree with the following statements? Have you or those who follow you expressed them?

- It is *acceptable* for a follower of Christ to attend a church for years and never make a commitment to it.
- It is *not* a violation of our allegiance to Christ to be baptized and take communion but never make a commitment to a local church.
- It is *not unbiblical* to be absent from church for weeks or months and to make major life decisions without consulting with others in the body of Christ.
- Loyalty to Jesus Christ *does not include* commitment to a local church.
- A healthy relationship with Jesus *does not have to include* a healthy relationship with His church.

Each of those statements uncovers a "Jesus and me" mindset. They expose leaders who are not in alignment with where the Scriptures say Jesus is working. They reveal leaders who are not treating Jesus's church as sacred. The statements ignore the fact that Jesus is chasing Hell back to its gates *through* His church, not apart from it.

JESUS SHAPES OUR CHARACTER THROUGH HIS FAMILY.

Jesus's second use of the word "church" makes crystal clear His intention to use His people to shape our character. As He says in Matthew 18:15–17, "If your brother sins, go and show him his fault in private; if he listens to you, you have won your brother. But if he does not listen to you, take one or two more with you, so that *by the mouth of two or three witnesses every fact may be confirmed.* If he refuses to listen to them, tell it to *the church*; and if he refuses to listen even to *the church*, let him be to you as a Gentile and a tax collector."

Jesus insists that His church is *a primary source* of "plugging the slow leaks" in our walk with Him. Being part of a community that loves each other enough to confront in a healthy and restorative way is essential to His plan for our growth in Him. The passage is built on an underlying assumption: His followers are so connected to each other that if one sins, all the others are impacted. Jesus's instructions are built on an implied mutual commitment to help each other walk in righteousness.

Jesus reveals how His church is to deal with sin in its members and outlines a clear, three-step process.

First, if your brother sins, go in private with the objective of helping to restore your brother (Matthew 18:15). Note that Jesus says, "if he listens to you." It takes courage and demonstrates love to first go in private to appeal to a sinning brother or sister. Doing this first also builds community because you are not telling others but going directly to the one who is at fault. The underlying assumption is that the church is a community that seeks to help each other walk in godliness.

Secondly, Jesus said, "If your brother will not hear you, then" (and only then) "take two or three with you" (Matthew 18:16). The objective is to confirm every fact and protect people's reputations. The underlying assumption is a community committed to not giving "bad reports" on each other. A bad report is sharing negative information about another to someone who does not need to hear the information. Jesus insists that the communication of negative information and confrontation not be expanded until going first in private to the one in sin.

Third, if the sinning brother will not listen to the appeal of the two or three witnesses who have confirmed the facts, then and only then are we to take it to the church (Matthew 18:17). Again, the implied motivation is to win your brother and pull him back into fellowship with Jesus and His people. If he refuses to listen to the church, then Jesus says, "let him be to you as a Gentile or tax collector."

What is the stance of the church toward those outside the faith—Gentiles and tax collectors? It is the same stance Jesus has: to seek to win them to Christ (Luke 19:10). At the same time, there is a clear recognition of lack of intimate fellowship with the church family until repentance takes place. If someone is adopted, they become a part of a new family. When we are adopted by Christ through faith in Him, we are also to be connected to His family. It is in the family that our character is shaped and deep love relationships are formed.

The next three verses, Matthew 18:18–20, win the prize for some of the most "quoted out of context" passages in the Bible.

It is important to realize who Jesus is speaking to so that the promises He makes are properly understood and applied. In Matthew18:18–20, Jesus gives assurance to those who are seeking to put into practice the ministry of restoration to those who refuse to repent and reconcile. If you have ever been engaged in this ministry of confrontation and restoration, you know that it can be intimidating. Note how Jesus reassures those engaged in the process:

Truly I say to you, whatever you bind on earth shall have been bound in heaven; and whatever you loose on earth shall have been loosed in heaven. Again I say to you, that if two of you agree on earth about anything that they may ask, it shall be done for them by My Father who is in heaven. **For where two or three have gathered together in My name, I am there in their midst.** (Emphasis mine.)

Jesus is addressing His disciples and passing along assurances to those involved in the process as well as the gathered church. When the church has heard the case against the sinning brother and appeals to repent have been rejected, the church is to regard that one as a Gentile or a tax collector. Jesus is assuring the church, "If you follow the process I have outlined, then you know that Heaven backs you. Whatever you (the church) have loosed or bound in the situation will have been also been loosed or bound in Heaven." In other words, Jesus works through His church to bring about discipline, which is to serve as a strong deterrent toward the slow leaks in our walk with God. The context makes clear that the "two or three" Jesus is referring to are those who have been involved in confirming facts and seeking to restore the sinning brother or sister.

According to Jesus, His church is both local and global and consists of people who confess Him as the Christ, the Son of the living God. His church is an invading force that will chase Hell back to its gates. His church is a community committed to joining Him in His work of healthy confrontation of sin and restoration to godly living. Is your life and leadership in alignment with what Jesus taught about His church?

WHAT DID GOD REVEAL TO PAUL ABOUT THE CHURCH?

The apostle Paul labored three years to establish the church in Ephesus (Acts 19:1–20:38). Paul's letter to them is a wonderful exposition on the spiritual riches *all* believers have because of their union with Jesus Christ (Ephesians 1:1–3:20) and how that union with Christ is to be expressed in our daily lives (Ephesians 4:1–6:23). The enjoyment and expression of these spiritual riches is intended to be enhanced in the context of a Christ-centered local church.

In Chapter 3, Paul uses the term "mystery" three times. This reveals the essential nature of the church (Ephesians 3:3, 4, 9). A mystery, as Paul uses it in this context, is referring to truth that was not revealed fully in the Old Testament but is now fully revealed in Jesus Christ. He makes clear that "the manifold wisdom of God might now be made known *through the church*" and "to Him who does more than we ask or think and his power works within us, to Him be glory *in the church*" (Ephesians 3:10, 21). The core mystery that is now revealed and accomplished in Christ is the mystery of the church: "that the Gentiles are fellow heirs and fellow members of the body, and fellow partakers of the promise in Christ Jesus through the gospel" (Ephesians 3:5–6). *Therefore, the church is made up of all people who have placed their faith in Jesus Christ for salvation.*

EPHESIANS 3 REVEALS FOUR ESSENTIAL ATTRIBUTES OF THE CHURCH OF JESUS CHRIST.

- It is *one* in Christ (made up of Jew and Gentile— Ephesians 3:6).

- It is *holy* (the dwelling place of God—Ephesians 3:19–20).
- It is *universal* (to Him be glory in the church to all generations—Ephesians 3:21).
- It is *apostolic* (founded on the apostles of Jesus and shaped by their teaching in the New Testament—Ephesians 3:5).

This essence was captured in the Nicene Creed (381 AD), which says; *"We believe in one holy catholic* (meaning universal) *apostolic church."*

The metaphors of the church, which Jesus and the apostles gave us, help us grasp God's intentions for her.

These describe the church universally as well as what should be reflected in local assemblies. One author identified over ninety of these metaphors, but six are the most examined in the New Testament: The church is a *body, bride, building, family, flock, and priesthood.*

- Jesus is the head of His *body*, the church, and each member has a unique function (1 Corinthians 12).
- The church is Jesus's beloved *bride* and shares life with Him (Ephesians 5; Revelations 19:7–10).
- Jesus is building His church into a holy *temple* in which He dwells (Ephesians 2:19–22).
- The church is a *family* in which every member matters and functions for the common good (2 Corinthians 6:16; Hebrews 8:10).
- Jesus is our high priest, and we are *believer priests* who worship and minister on Jesus's behalf (Hebrews 7:25; 1 Peter 2:9).

Therefore, a Christian and especially a ministry leader without a church is a contradiction. It would be like an arm trying to function without connecting to the torso under submission to the head. It would be like saying, "I am a bride, but I don't have a husband." Does your leadership reflect Jesus's intentions for His church?

Doctor Luke rounds out our study of the church. His accurate record of its early history is preserved for us in the New Testament book of Acts. He records the essential traits that healthy local churches have been exhibiting ever since.

ESSENTIAL TRAITS OF A HEALTHY CHURCH

John the Baptist proclaimed that Jesus would baptize with the Holy Spirit those who believed in Him as Messiah (Matthew 3:11; Mark 1:8; Luke 3:16; John 1:33). Jesus promised that after his ascension to the Father, the Holy Spirit would come upon His followers (Acts 1:4–5).

The baptism of the Holy Spirit, which occurred on Pentecost, was like a *reverse* tower of Babel (Acts 2:1–11; Genesis 11). At Babel, the people *scattered* because God confused their languages. At Pentecost, the people *gathered* because each heard God's praises in their own native tongue (Acts 2:7–12). This was the birthday and empowering of the church for its mission; to make disciples of all peoples. (Acts 1:8; Matthew 28:18–20). On that day when Peter stood and proclaimed the Gospel, Luke tells us,

So then, those who had received his word were baptized; and that day there were added about three thousand souls. They were continually devoting themselves to the apostles' teaching and to fellowship, to the breaking of bread and to prayer. Everyone kept feeling a sense of awe; and many wonders and signs were taking place through the apostles. And all those who had believed were together and had all things in common; and they began selling their property and possessions and were sharing them with all, as anyone might have need. Day by day continuing with one mind in the temple, and breaking bread from house to house, they were taking their meals together with gladness and sincerity of heart, praising God and having favor with all the people. And the Lord was adding to their number day by day those who were being saved.

Did you notice the pattern in verse 41? *Receive the word* (believe the Gospel of Jesus Christ), be *baptized,* and then be *added* to the church. This pattern provides us with **the first essential of our definition of a local church:** *It consists of baptized believers in Jesus Christ.*

Another essential is revealed in verses 42–46. Are you in the habit of gathering with other believers? Is this a priority in your life? Did you know one of the strongest warnings of God's severe discipline is because believers neglect coming together with other believers? We find that in the book of Hebrews: *"not forsaking our own assembling together,* as is the habit of some, but encouraging one another; and all the more as you see the day drawing near. *For if we go on sinning willfully* after receiving the knowledge of the truth, there no longer remains a sacrifice for sins, but a terrifying expectation of judgment and *the fury of a fire which will consume the adversaries"* (Hebrews 10:25–27). The practice of the early church provides **the next essential of a local church:** *habitually gathering together.*

Acts 2:42 reminds us that the church was not without qualified leaders. Peter and the apostles were qualified to lead because they had been chosen and trained by Jesus Christ. After a vast number believed the Gospel, Peter preached, and they continued to devote themselves to the apostles' teachings. As the church spread among the Gentiles, they appointed elders, overseers, and pastors to lead the local churches. The three titles describe different aspects of the same office (Acts 20:17, 28). Elders indicate spiritual maturity. Overseers indicate the role of leaders. Shepherds or pastors indicate the call to care for God's flock and feed them on God's word. Paul clarified the qualifications for these leaders in 1 Timothy 3:1–7, Titus 1:5–9, 1 Peter 5:1–5, and Acts 20:13–38.[4] Thus, **the third essential in our definition of a local church is that it is *led by qualified shepherds*.**

Acts 2:47 indicates that the church was a worshiping community. What an amazing and life-giving atmosphere of full participation in worship—they were praising God, having favor with all people, and the Lord was adding day by day to their number those who were being saved. **This is the fourth essential of a healthy local church: *Participatory worship of the Triune God*.**

The teaching of the apostles has been preserved for us in the New Testament, which points back to and demonstrates the fulfillment of the Old Testament in Jesus Christ (John 5:39; Luke 24:44). This is the lifeblood of the church. The Bible calls it *sound* or *hygienic* doctrine and *the faith* (1 Timothy 1:10, 4:16, 6:3; Titus 1:9, 2:1). **Therefore, our fifth essential of a healthy church is consistent *study and application of the Scriptures*.**

The consistent pattern in the New Testament is that once someone places their faith in Jesus Christ for salvation, they are baptized and then added to the church. Verse 42 says "they were *breaking bread together*" and verse 46 says "they were *taking their meals together*." Many believe the meals included communion, or the Lord's Supper, which Jesus had commanded them to do in remembrance of Him (Matthew 26:26–30; Mark 14:22–26; Luke 22:14–23; John 13:1–20). Paul recalls Jesus's commands and outlines the proper way to observe communion in 1 Corinthians 11:23–34. The Reformers taught that the church is to be marked by rightly teaching the Scriptures and rightly practicing the sacraments of baptism and communion. **Therefore, our sixth essential of a healthy church is that** *it observes baptism and communion.*

Finally, verses 44–47 describe the vibrant life of the church which God was working in and through to accomplish His purposes: "And all those who had believed were together and had all things in common; and they began selling their property and possessions and were sharing them with all, as anyone might have need. Day by day continuing with one mind in the temple, and breaking bread from house to house, they were taking their meals together with gladness and sincerity of heart, praising God and having favor with all the people. And the Lord was adding to their number day by day those who were being saved."

Jesus had commanded them to obey the Great Command to love God and people above all else (Matthew 22:37–40) and the Great Commission—to make disciples of all peoples (Matthew 28:18–20). This vibrant community was engaged in making disciples and loving God and each other. This resulted in glorifying God; He was being praised through them, and He was adding to their number those who were being saved. The church functioned as prongs on a diamond, displaying the beauty of Jesus Christ. The pattern they cut along is the same one we are to follow for the glory of God. Therefore, **the seventh essential of a healthy church is that** it *obeys the Great Command and the Great Commission for the glory of God.*

Our journey with Jesus, Paul, and Luke has equipped us to clearly define the essentials of a healthy local church. This is important because our task as ministry leaders is to know this essential biblical definition and use it as a grid to align ourselves and those we lead with God's purposes.

These essentials are gleaned directly from the Scriptures and can be applied in thousands of ways across the world in vastly different context and cultures. No more assumptions! No more vague answers about what Jesus is building and what He wants His church to look like!

> *A local church consists of baptized believers in Jesus Christ, connected to the global body of Christ, who habitually gather under the leadership of qualified shepherds to worship the Triune God, study and apply the Scriptures, practice baptism and communion, and obey the Great Command and the Great Commission for the glory of God.*

This is what Jesus is building! Ministry leaders who intentionally align their lives with what Jesus is building are on the path to thriving and finishing strong.

MY CONFESSION

There was a long season in my life in which I slowly developed a dreary view of pastors and merely tolerated the local church. To me, ministers seemed to be sidelined from actively engaging the world. I thought their lives were consumed with conducting "less than compelling" religious services, giving irrelevant talks on Sundays, putting up with disgruntled church members, attending boring meetings, and running outdated religious institutions. I did not hate the church. I attended weekly, benefited from its programs, and appreciated its service to the community.

However, I did somewhat disdain the church and its leaders. As I write, I am aware of how arrogant it sounds, but this is a confession, so I am coming clean. I did not associate churches and their leaders with making a radical difference in the world, and I never linked them with adventure.

Therefore, the last thing I ever wanted to be was a pastor of a local church. My adventure with Christ was found outside the church in the hands-on ministry of introducing people to Him, helping them reach others, and launching Gospel movements on college campuses. I "came alive" in college through the training of Campus Crusade for Christ (now known as Cru). Therefore, after graduating with a business degree, I joined their staff and was assigned to Auburn University in Alabama. My two years on staff were some of the most fulfilling of my life. I loved ever nanosecond! The results of leading people to Christ, equipping them in the context of a small group, and empowering them to reach others have lasted to this day. Scores of ministry leaders serve around the world today because of the radical difference Christ made in their lives through my ministry in partnership with Cru.

In this context, I met a captivating young lady named Mae Belle Annandale. I was captured by her godly character, sweet Southern voice, intelligence, faithfulness to her five younger siblings, and passion for Christ. I learned that her heritage was sourced in a long line of godly women who were also named Mae Belle. She is the fifth and final Mae Belle in a long line of godly Mae Belles!

When Mae Belle and I became serious about our relationship and made plans for marriage, her mother Mae Belle and grandmother Mae Belle went to work. These two godly women joined forces and began to pray daily for me. They clearly communicated the specific content of their fervent petitions to God: "We think you should resign from Cru, go to seminary, and become the pastor of a local church." I made crystal clear my complete lack of desire to step out of the "front lines of ministry" and spend three to four years in seminary so that I could be "qualified" to be "relegated to the sidelines" as a pastor in a local church. The harder I resisted the "Mae Belle pleas," the more intensely they prayed and appealed to me. Their prayers set the stage for my lasting encounter with God.

During my second year on Cru staff, I was opening campus ministries on dozens of college campuses in southern Alabama. I was having the time of my life and was dreaming of a bright future with Cru. Yet God was about to get my attention, alter my perspective, and place me on a new path.

One of my co-laborers gave me a series of messages by a pastor in California. As I traveled the back roads of Alabama and enjoyed launching movements of the Gospel on college campuses, I repeatedly listened to them.

The pastor I was listening to immediately destroyed my negative stereotype of pastors. He was adventurous, courageous, and compelling. Beyond that, he was convinced by Scripture that God's priority is the local church. His captivating and careful exposition of 1 and 2 Timothy convinced me that my perceptions of the church were out of touch with God's view. I was deeply convicted that I had been despising Jesus's "blood-bought bride" and the shepherds He put in place to care for His flock.

I was a ministry leader and doing God's work, but I had spiritual Lowell's syndrome when it came to the truth about Jesus's church. I needed to stop discounting the beautiful body of Christ and realign my thinking with the truth about Jesus's heart for His church.

I became consumed with a deep hunger to know God's Word and longed to learn how to clearly and compellingly communicate it. *My views of the local church shifted from being shaped by my experiences to being formed by what God's Word says about the bride of Christ.* A growing passion began to drive me. I wanted to be equipped to lead a local church in line with God's clear instructions in the New Testament.

All the Mae Belles rejoiced when I shared this news and ramped up their prayers for me! My local church confirmed my new calling, licensed me to the gospel ministry, encouraged me to go to seminary and urged me to pursue becoming a pastor. I resigned from Cru (I still love and appreciate their vital ministry), was accepted at Western Seminary in Portland, Oregon, and married my sweetheart.

Western equipped me to effectively expound and apply God's Word and solidified in me Bible-based convictions regarding the priority of the local church in fulfilling God's kingdom purposes. My final year in seminary, I was called to be the senior pastor of the local church I was attending, and I had the joy of leading that congregation for seven fruitful years. Mae Belle and I, along with our two sons Joshua and Caleb, moved to Arlington, Virginia, in 1983, and I became the senior pastor of Cherrydale Baptist Church. I have had the joy of serving this flourishing flock for over thirty-five years.

I can honestly say after four decades of ministry that serving Jesus Christ *through His church* has been the adventure of a lifetime! I believe Christ-centered, Gospel-shaped, biblically fed and led local churches are the hope of the world! I constantly associate local churches with making a radical difference in the world and link them with adventure. I have never looked back from God's call to me on the back roads of Alabama. Yes, I have faced a thousand quitting points, been deeply hurt and devastatingly disappointed. However, I have learned to align my life with what Jesus is building and have discovered that He is faithful to empower me to thrive and finish strong.

WHAT ABOUT YOU?

You may not be called to be a pastor or a leader in a local church, but if you are reading this book, you are most likely a ministry leader of some kind and a follower of Jesus Christ. Therefore, God is calling you to honor His bride and align your life with His purposes through her.

Jesus is relentless in His quest to mold us into His image (Romans 8:28–29). His primary agent is what He died for, lives in, works through, prays for, is perfecting, is coming back for, and will spend eternity delighting in—His church.

His way of delivering us from spiritual Lowell's syndrome regarding His church is to get our attention, alter our views with His truth, and give us an assignment.

Jesus Gets Our Attention → Alters Our Views → Gives Us an Assignment

This three-fold pattern is woven through the stories of the main characters of the Bible. Therefore, we can anticipate that God will cut along the same pattern when He moves to shape *our* lives. He is speaking. Are you listening?

WORKOUTS TO THRIVE AND FINISH STRONG

A. Write out your answers to the following questions and take specific action, in the power of the Holy Spirit, to alter your views and fulfill your God-given assignments.

What is your story with the church?

Have you lost heart and drifted away because you can't find what you have been looking for?

Have you been wounded by the church? Have you responded by creating your own path for growth in Christ, a path that does not include the bride of Christ?

Are you willing to let God speak to you through His Word regarding His church and take some specific actions to align your life with it?

The church is Jesus's treasure. Do you treasure what Jesus does? Why or why not?

B. Review the following reasons and accompanying scripture for making a commitment to a local church.

Commitment to a church is the biblical pattern. Acts 2:41–42; Hebrews 10:19–25

A church is God's provision for your growth in Christ. Ephesians 4:11–12; 2 Corinthians 8–9

Commitment to a church is how you join Jesus in His work. Matthew 16:18; 28:18–20

Commitment to a church glorifies God. John 13:34–35; 1 Peter 2:8–9

C. Confess your sins toward Jesus and His church. Be specific in your confession and repent.

D. Read at least one of the recommended sources, review this chapter, and share the one-page summary below with a friend.

What is a local church?

> *A local church consists of baptized believers in Jesus Christ, connected to the global body of Christ, who habitually gather under the leadership of qualified shepherds to worship the Triune God, study and apply the Scriptures, practice baptism and communion, and obey the Great Command and the Great Commission for the glory of God.*

Scriptures

- Matthew 16:13–19; 18:15–20
- Ephesians 3:1–21
- Acts 2:37–47
- Other key passages: Acts 2, 15, 20; 1 Corinthians 12, and 1 Peter 5.
- Primary New Testament books regarding the church: Acts, Ephesians, 1 and 2 Timothy and Titus.

Metaphors of the church

- Body—1 Corinthians 12:12–27
- Bride—Ephesians 5:32; 2 Corinthians 11:2
- Building—Ephesians 1; 1 Corinthians 3:9; 1 Peter 2:5
- Family—1 Timothy 5:1–2; Ephesians 3:14; 2 Corinthians 6:18; 1 John 3:14–18; Matthew 12:49–50
- Priesthood—1 Peter 2:5–9
- Flock—John 10
- Branches in the Vine—John 15

CHAPTER 4

Let the Grace of God Instruct You

The evidence that a leader has been amazed by grace is that he or she is continually instructed by it.

A re you a grace-instructed leader?

Do you know how to tell if you are?

Are you amazed by the grace of God?

Your answer to those three questions reveals if you are on the way to thriving and finishing well as a leader. It is *essential* that you learn to let the grace of God instruct you.

"I have never gotten over the *thrill* of learning that I am justified before God through faith in Jesus Christ. This is *astounding* to me![1] Justified means you stand before God just as if you never sinned *and* just as if everything you did was righteous! That is how God views you if you are in Christ. So how can I, being justified by grace, turn around and self-righteously damn other sinners instead of loving them as God loved me?"

I preached those words to my church family six years ago, and I followed with a confession.

"We need to get the truth of justification down into our hearts. I became a Christian at the age of nine. I now am sixty-five years old, and I have an issue I have struggled with my whole Christian life. I will probably die struggling with it, but it is getting better as I learn how to get this truth of justification by grace in my heart.

"You are wondering, 'What is your issue?' I am glad you asked! I have an anger problem. Whenever I feel disregarded or disrespected, it pushes my buttons! How would this truth of justification help me? Here is how it helps me. I am trying to implant this wonderful truth into my heart and mind. I talk the Gospel to myself: 'Steve, if you are so upset that you are disregarded or disrespected, hello! The God of the universe *never* disregards you. You have all the respect you can dream of *in Christ*. So, let it go!' That helps me."

Dozens have come to me for help with their anger issues since that confession about mine and how God's grace is instructing me and helping me. As a matter of fact, a member who moved to another state made an appointment with me just this past Saturday to talk about his anger issue because he heard me make this confession *six years ago*. When others saw me being instructed by grace, they were compelled to join me in the journey.

Being instructed by God's grace is painful, at times humiliating, and requires repentance. You can't be a grace-instructed leader unless you are willing to get off the throne of your life and fully yield yourself to Jesus. When leaders let the grace of

God instruct them, their leadership goes *beyond* human limitations to God's power.

Being a leader who lets the grace of God instruct you *begins* with being amazed by it.

It continues as you intentionally learn to let God's grace amaze you. God's grace is in Christ as taught by the Scriptures, and it is expressed to us through others who have been amazed by it.

GRACE WITH A FACE

I was profoundly awakened to the reality of God's grace by a grace-instructed leader. My journey toward the awakening was preceded by plunging headfirst into many foolish quests during my growing-up years. However, the mother of them all occurred when I was fifteen.

My generous father helped me and my older sister, Judy, acquire our first car. It was a 1957 Ford with a 280 horsepower V-8 engine, and we thought it was the best automobile ever. I had a learner's license, and my older sister had a legitimate one. Therefore, I could only drive the car when my sister or another licensed driver was with me. Each day, my sister would drive us to school. I enjoyed revving the engine for my friends and bragging about the power under the hood.

One day, I said to my friend David, "Would you like to skip school at lunchtime and go for a ride in my car?" He eagerly agreed, so we ran across the parking lot, hopped into my "hot rod," and took a spin in the country.

Once we were a safe distance from school and on an abandoned road, I decided to show David what my car could do. My automobile had an automatic transmission, and I wanted to show my friend how I could make it "burn rubber." I put the car in neutral, revved the engine and then shifted it into drive. But instead of hearing squealing tires and smelling burnt rubber, we saw smoke coming from under the hood! The force of moving quickly from neutral to drive with the engine revving at high speed caused the engine to lock. The car "went to be with the Lord" right on the spot!

I said to my friend, "If you ever tell on me for what I am about to do, I will kill you." I was kidding, of course, but he got the point: Keep your mouth shut! I then asked him to help me push the car into a ditch so it would look like it had been wrecked. We hitchhiked back to school with a farmer.

By then, school was nearly over for the day, and I had some explaining to do regarding my car. I lied to the principal, police officers, my sister, my friends, and to my dad. I told them all, "Someone stole my car!" Later that afternoon, my cousin and I just "happened" to find my "stolen treasure" on the side of a country road.

My father never questioned me. He was the district manager of the Goodyear stores in the region and had my car towed to a nearby shop. He paid his best mechanic to put a new engine in the car and gave it back to me and my sister.

My conscience was killing me, but I refused to come clean, and my friend never said a word. Years went by, and the pain of my deception was eating a hole in my soul. Finally, I mustered my courage and asked my dad if he would go on a walk with me.

I told him about my deception and how sorry I was for what I had done. What my father did next will forever be etched in my mind.

He stopped walking, turned to me, put his hands on my shoulders, looked me in the eye and said, "Look at me."

I immediately obeyed. He then said, "I have two things to say to you. Number one, I knew the whole time. Number two, I forgive you."

I was so overcome by his amazing grace that I began to sob. He never mentioned it again, and he never asked me to pay for my evil deed. His forgiveness was complete and authentic. I was amazed at his grace.

- My dad knew all about my evil deception, yet he patiently waited for me to repent. Our heavenly Father does the same for us.
- While my dad waited for me to come clean, he continued to show me grace and paid the price for my sin at his own expense. Our heavenly Father has done the same for us in Christ.
- When I finally admitted my sins, my dad made it crystal clear that he forgave me. He withheld from me the punishment I deserved and provided for me what I was unworthy to receive. Our heavenly Father does the same for us when we repent and trust in Christ.

Dad's favor to me was undeserved and costly to him. It reflected the Sunday School definition of God's grace to us in Christ: **G**od's **R**iches **a**t **C**hrist's **E**xpense. When Dad "graced me," I couldn't help but think, *So, this is what God's grace is like!*

I was being instructed by grace!

First, it taught me to *say no to sin;* I never deceived him again, and my foolish quests ended.

Second, it taught me to *say yes to God*; His grace became a powerful force which motivated me to mind the major leaks in my character.

Third, it taught me to *hope in God*. That day on the sidewalk with my dad, it was as if God took a funnel and poured His love and forgiveness into my heart and compelled me to hope in Him.

Grace-instructed leaders are part of a chain reaction that goes from generation to generation!

That day, *I* was instructed by grace through my grace-instructed *father* who had been instructed in grace by *another* grace-instructed leader.

When my dad was nine, he was devastated by the death of his own father, who was handsome, full of life, and drank heavily. While out on a hunting trip, he fell off a cliff in a drunken stupor. He broke his leg and soon thereafter died of gangrene. His wife was left to raise my dad and his older sister on her own. She favored the older sister and disdained my dad because he looked like her dead husband.

A grace-instructed pastor in the community heard about this devastated family and reached out to them. He led them to Christ and invested in my dad and a dozen other boys in the community. Through the pastor's influence, my dad learned about the grace of God in Christ and became a grace-instructed leader.

As a leader, consider the generational impact God wants to unleash through you as you are instructed by grace.

The evidence that we have been amazed by the grace of God is that we let it instruct us.

God's grace *always* instructs us and moves us to mind the slow leaks in our character. Paul's letter to Titus makes this crystal clear:

*For **the grace of God** has appeared, bringing salvation to all men, **instructing us** to deny ungodliness and worldly desires and to live sensibly, righteously and godly in the present age, looking for the blessed hope and the appearing of the glory of our great God and Savior, Christ Jesus, who gave Himself for us to redeem us from every lawless deed, and to purify for Himself a people for His own possession, zealous for good deeds* (Titus 2:11–14, emphasis mine).

Paul longed for Titus to be a grace-instructed leader who would be used by God to multiply many other grace-instructed leaders. He provides Titus a treasure chest of "grace-truth" in this passage.

- *First*, he says the grace of God has *appeared*. It has been made visible in the person and work of Jesus Christ.
- *Second*, grace brings with it the offer of *salvation* to all people; again, based on the work of Jesus Christ on our behalf.
- Pay close attention to the *third* insight about grace Paul gave Titus; it lets us know how to tell if we are grace-instructed leaders. Paul says grace *instructs* us to *deny* ungodliness, to *live* righteously, and to *hope* in the coming of Christ.

The grace of God *always* instructs with a three-fold emphasis: say no to sin, yes to God, and hope in His coming Kingdom. The lives of grace-instructed leaders *always* bear these traits.

GRACE-INSTRUCTED LEADERS SAY NO

We are to say no to what is not like Jesus Christ—what is ungodly. In addition, we are also to turn our back to worldly desires. The word translated "desires" is from the Greek word *epithumia*. *Epi* is an intensive and *thumia* is "desire"; thus, the word means "excessive desires." The Greek word for "worldly" is *cosmos* and refers to a well-ordered system. According to 1 John 2:16, worldliness consists of three passions in each of us: "All that is in the world, *the lust of the flesh* and *the lust of the eyes* and *the boastful pride of life*, is not from the Father, but from the world." These same three were at the root of the temptation Adam and Eve faced in Eden (Genesis 3:6).

My friend Jay Carty, a former starter for the LA Lakers who turned evangelist and is now in Heaven, used to lead "Big Three" workshops. His exposition of these three descriptors of worldliness and the accompanying insights on how to defeat them in Christ had a lasting impact on me. I summarize some of his insights below:

The lust of the flesh is a natural desire aimed in the wrong direction. For example, it is not sinful, in and of itself, to want to eat or have sex. However, God has put guardrails around both; don't be a glutton (1 Corinthians 10:7; Philippians 3:19) and do not participate in sex outside of your own marriage (1 Thessalonians 4:1–8). The lust of the flesh pushes past those boundaries and becomes sin.

The lust of the eyes means to long for what you have no right to. It is not wrong to enjoy looking at so many wonderful things in the world. It *is* wrong to covet your neighbor's wife, house, car, etc. (Exodus 20:17). "Lust of the eyes" means that you want all you see without restraint.

The boastful pride of life is pride in possessions. It means that you build your identity on *temporary* possessions. It means that you refuse to build your identity on what you can never lose—being created in the image of God and your identity in Christ. The boastful pride of life can turn us into racists, social snobs, and self-righteous Pharisees. If we reject God's moral standards, revealed in both our conscience and the Bible, we are left adrift with no way to define ungodliness, worldly desires, or lusts. When we understand the grace of God, grasp how much God loves us in Christ, and start to comprehend who we are in Him, we will say no to ungodliness and worldly desires.

Leaders need to be aware of the subtle tugs of the "Big Three." Miss this, and you will not be a grace-instructed leader.

Political persuasions that become too attached to our faith can be dangerous and feed the pride of life. Yes, hold biblical convictions without apology, but do not align a political party with your faith. Don't forget that, as followers of Christ, we are not elephants or donkeys but sheep. Our full allegiance belongs only to Christ. How do you know if you are members of the same body with someone else? You both have the same head! Our head is Jesus Christ, not a political party.

Grace-instructed leaders need to model and teach the clear instructions in Titus 3:1–2: "Remind them to be subject to rulers, to authorities, to be obedient, to be ready for every good deed, *to malign no one, to be peaceable, gentle, showing every consideration for all men.*" Do you have certain people in the culture that you label as "they," whom you cannot speak of without disdain? I pray to God that one day people will view followers of Christ as Titus 3:2 kind of people!

As grace-instructed leaders, we are to reprove but *never* revile. "Reprove" means to confront in love for the purpose of restoring someone who has gone astray. "Revile" means to repeat the vile, to accuse and malign with no intention of restoring.

Many leaders are rightly concerned with the moral boundaries around sex being so rapidly moved. Grace-instructed leaders approach the issue by remembering that we are *all* sexually broken and need grace for healing. Refusing to begin here indicates that the pride of life may have blinded you.

Recently, one of my friends who is a pastor was reading his Bible in a restaurant booth. A young man approached him and saw it. He said, "I hate that book. I am a homosexual, and it condemns me." My friend wisely and graciously responded, "I love this book. I am a heterosexual and it condemns me, too." His response surprised the young man, and it led to a healthy conversation in which my friend was able to share the Gospel with him.

Pastor Ken Smith is another grace-instructed leader. Ask Rosaria Butterfield.[2] She was a lesbian, agnostic English professor in Syracuse, New York, who was researching why the "religious right" hates gays. She wrote an article expressing her views in her local newspaper. In response, she received some hate mail, some letters from people supportive of her views, and a few letters from people who disagreed with her in a gracious way. Smith's response stunned her because he totally disagreed with her but did so with grace, humility, and good questions. Smith and his wife formed a friendship with Rosaria and her gay community. Rosaria was converted to Christ, embraced a biblical sexual ethic, and is now the wife of a pastor.

Ed Shaw is another courageous leader who is intentionally being instructed by grace against the big three of 1 John 2:16. He is a single, celibate, evangelical pastor with same-sex attraction. He longs to demonstrate with his life and through his local church the surprising plausibility of the celibate life. His insightful book outlines nine missteps evangelical leaders have made in contending for the truth about sexuality.[3]

Megachurch pastors Bill Hybels and James MacDonald have been disciplined and removed from the local churches they founded and faithfully labored in for years. The seeds of compromise they sowed along the way came to light, and the warning of Galatians 6:7 proved true: "Do not be deceived, God is not mocked; for whatever a man sows, this he will also reap." Why not stop right now and intercede for these brothers in Christ and let their lives be a firm warning to beware the slow leaks in our own lives?

GRACE-INSTRUCTED LEADERS SAY YES

God's grace instructs us to *live* sensibly and righteously. These terms describe the character of Jesus Christ. God's grace *always* instructs us both negatively and positively; it compels us to say *no* to sin and *yes* to God—to *die* to our old life without Christ and *live* our new life in Christ. It calls us to practice a Good Friday and an Easter Sunday lifestyle.

On the first day of 2019, I got up and read the Sermon on the Mount. A freshness about Jesus, Who is calling me to say yes to Him, captured me. His sermon was addressed to His disciples, yet the crowds listened in (Matthew 5:1–2, 7:28–29).

The crowds were *astonished* at His teaching because it carried authority. As I read, I found myself astonished at His teaching too! Jesus spoke *as God in the flesh*, clearly stated who would be blessed and why, and assured them of what only God could assure them of—who will enter the Kingdom of Heaven (5:3–10)!

He declared *Himself* to be superior to the Law and all the prophets because both would be fulfilled only *in Him* (5:11–17).

He had the audacity to declare that His disciples have a radical new identity as salt and light *because* they believed in *Him* (5:13–14)!

He insisted that *He alone* would fulfill the Law, and he had the gall to make Himself *the final authority on truth* (5:17–26).

He revealed things *only* God could know—what is in the human heart and who goes to Heaven or Hell (5:18–48)!

He spoke *as man's final judge* and declared who would be rewarded and who would not (6:1–34).

He gave absolute instructions on human relationship *as if He were man's Creator* and closed His sermon by *declaring Himself the Lord* before Whom all would stand in judgment (7:1–23).

He closed by insisting that only those who say yes *to Him* (hear and obey *His Word*) will be stable, and all others will be swept away in the storm of God's judgment.

Wow! Talk about the grace of God instructing me to say yes to Jesus! Who else but Jesus would I dare turn the control of my life over to?

Few people know of the two sisters who said *yes* to the call of Jesus Christ and shared the Gospel with generations of West Point cadets—including future U.S. President Dwight D. Eisenhower. Susan and Anna Warner never married, but they lived on the island across from West Point and provided for themselves by writing. Susan produced a novel per year; her first, *The Wide, Wide Word,* was second only in sales and popularity to *Uncle Tom's Cabin* in 1899. Anna also wrote many popular books and was the author of the famous hymn, "Jesus Loves Me." For over forty years, cadets would row to their island home on Sunday afternoons to participate in a Bible study. They are the only two civilian women buried in the West Point cemetery, and "Jesus Loves Me" has become one of the theme songs of the Protestant chapel.[4]

GRACE-INSTRUCTED LEADERS HOPE

God's grace instructs us to *hope*. Our hope is in the appearing of Jesus Christ, who will come back and restore all that was lost in mankind's fall into sin. Paul refers to Jesus as *"our great God and Savior, Christ Jesus, who gave Himself for us."* The only God with scars and blood on His body is the God made flesh in Jesus Christ.

God's grace instruction is linked to His Word. The degree to which we study, apply, and absorb ourselves in God's Word is the degree to which we will experience God's grace instruction. Show me a leader who is not immersed in God's Word, and I will show you a leader who is not being instructed in the grace of God.

A DIVINELY INSPIRED MANUAL

Hebrews is one of my go-to books for becoming a grace-instructed leader. Its unknown yet divinely inspired author wrote it as a letter to Hebrews (Jews for Jesus) who were suffering for their faith in Christ. *The cure* for their temptation to drift away, become dull of hearing, and lose heart was *instruction by the grace of God.*

The author only mentions grace six times, yet the instructions of grace are woven through the fabric of the book. He instructs us to *hope* in Jesus Christ, *live* a new life in Him, and *deny* ungodliness. The author calls his work an exhortation and *begins and ends* by urging us to listen to the God who is speaking in Jesus Christ (Hebrews 1:1–3; 12:25; 13:22). Hope in Christ is insisted on with three key words: "better," "perfect," and "eternal."

Better is sprinkled through the book thirteen times and is used to declare the superiority of Jesus Christ. Savor what you are about to read about Jesus. If your fascination with Him has waned, then ask God to renew your hope in Him as you review why He is the ultimate *better than* all others!

He is better than the prophets because He inspired and fulfilled their message (Hebrews 1:1–3).

He is better than the angels because He created them and they worship Him (Hebrews 1:4–2:18).

He is better than Moses because He is the better leader, law-giver and overseer of His house (Hebrews 3:1–6).

He is better than Aaron because He offered the final sacrifice for sins and is the Eternal High Priest (Hebrews 5:1–10).

He has a better covenant because it is new and fulfills and replaces the old one (Hebrews 8:1–13).

He is the better sanctuary because He is the true one (Hebrews 9:1–27).

He offered the better sacrifice by which He perfected forever those who believe in Him (Hebrews 10:1–25).

Perfect is "perfectly" inserted through the book fourteen times. Jesus is the perfect author of our salvation, made perfect forever, entered the more perfect tabernacle for us, and makes us perfect forever by His one sacrifice for our sins (Hebrews 5:9, 7:28, 9:11, 10:14, 12:23).

Eternal is linked to Jesus Christ because He is the source of eternal salvation, has obtained eternal redemption for us, and has shed His blood so we could enjoy the eternal covenant with God (Hebrews 5:9; 9:12, 15; 13:20).

Review this often and let God's amazing grace in Christ instruct you!

Hebrews instructs leaders to embrace assurance of salvation. God's grace is extravagant!

Passages on the assurance of salvation run like a life-giving stream through the book and are given to fortify our confidence in the work of Christ on our behalf. They provide a sure foundation that is designed to accelerate our growth in Christ—to provoke us to beware slow leaks!

Consider the strong *assurance of salvation promises*:

1. Jesus, the author of our salvation, will bring us to glory and calls us brethren (Hebrews 2:10–11).
2. Jesus makes propitiation (complete satisfaction) for the sins of the people (Hebrews 2:17).
3. Believers are called holy and partakers of a heavenly calling (Hebrews 3:1).
4. Christ is faithful over His house ("whose house *we are*" (Hebrews 3:6).
5. We have become partakers of Christ (Hebrews 3:14).
6. We have a great high priest and can draw near with confidence to the throne of grace (Hebrews 4:14–16).
7. Jesus is the source of our *eternal* salvation (Hebrews 5:9).
8. Our hope in Christ is *the* anchor of our soul; He is sure and steadfast (Hebrews 6:19).
9. Jesus is our eternal high priest, can *save us forever*, and always lives to make intercession for us (Hebrews 7:24–25).
10. We are partakers of a new covenant with better promises (Hebrews 8:6).
11. Christ obtained *eternal* redemption for us, we have and *eternal* inheritance, He appears in the presence of God for us, and put away our sin by sacrificing Himself (Hebrews 9:12, 15, 24, 26).
12. By His one sacrifice for our sins, He has *perfected us for all time* (Hebrews 10:14).

13. *We have* confidence to enter God's presence, and we have a high priest in Jesus (Hebrews 10:19–21).
14. We gain approval before God by our faith (Hebrews 11:39–40).
15. Jesus is the author and perfecter of our faith (Hebrews 12:2).
16. We are God's sons, and His discipline demonstrates our sonship (Hebrews 12:7–8).
17. Believers in Christ are enrolled in Heaven and called the righteous, made perfect (Hebrews 12:22–23).
18. We receive a kingdom which cannot be shaken (Hebrews 12:28).
19. He promises that He will never desert us or ever forsake us (Hebrews 13:5).
20. He is working in us to do what is pleasing in His sight (Hebrews 13:21).

Yet Hebrews will not let us settle for "cheap grace" by dissecting its assurance of salvation promises from its demands of obedience. It is one of the most affirming books in the New Testament on assurance of eternal life in Christ, yet it contains some of the most severe warnings to those who have "fallen away," "insulted the Spirit of grace," and "come short" of the grace of God.

Hebrews provides us an assurance that accelerates our growth in Christ. This grace-saturated manual insists that instruction in grace is essential to beware the slow leaks in our lives!

Hebrews instructs leaders to anticipate relentless discipline—God's discipline is extensive!

The inspired author of Hebrews presents a paradigm that unlocks the apparent conflict between God's extravagantly assuring grace and His extensive discipline. Understanding this paradigm will accelerate your growth as a grace-instructed leader. Master this and let it shape your commitment to be a grace-instructed leader.

I made some fascinating discoveries as I saturated myself in the book of Hebrews. This grace-instructing manual is a treasure chest! Hebrews was written to motivate us to pay close attention to the God who is speaking to us in Jesus Christ (Hebrews 1:1–3; 2:1–2; 12:25). Its forty-four exhortations function much like a coach or trainer who constantly urges us to diligently claim God's promises.

As I repeatedly read through the book, I noted a pattern which I have labeled "The 32/18 Principle." The book contains *thirty-two joys or benefits* which accompany treasuring Christ. Some examples are confidence in God, healthy relationships, assurance of salvation, rest in your soul, discernment, clean conscience, freedom from materialism, and the ability to break through quitting points. It also contains *eighteen sorrows that accompany unbelief.* These few examples are strong motivators to repent: you will no longer hear God's voice, your heart will be hardened, you will be deceived, you will waste your life, you will lack wisdom, you will grieve the heart of God, and you will be discontent. The complete 32/18 Principle is provided in the appendix.

The author of Hebrews also provides a paradigm that will clarify how the strong assurance of salvation verses walk hand-in-hand with the five increasingly severe warning passages. Hebrew believers would have understood the paradigm, but we in the Western world can easily overlook it. The paradigm is especially evident in Hebrews 3 and 4 but forms a backdrop for the entire book.

The author refers to three geographical locations that were part of the history of God's people: *Egypt,* where they were enslaved for four hundred years; *the wilderness,* where they wandered for forty years; and *the Promised Land,* which they entered under the leadership of Joshua. These three geographical locations and what happened in each parallel the experiences of all believers in Christ. So do not write yourself out of this story—this will clarify how God's extravagant grace is welded to His extensive discipline in each of our lives.

Egypt is where God's people were enslaved and oppressed, and the only way out of the situation was divine intervention. God sent Moses to champion their cause, along with ten plagues which culminated with the Passover. God led the children of Israel by the pillar of fire and cloud until they came to the Red Sea, and then He destroyed the Egyptian army in it. Egypt represents our lost state without Christ; we are enslaved to sin, and our only hope is divine intervention. God sent "the greater than Moses" Jesus Christ, who became our Passover Lamb and transferred us from the domain of darkness into the Kingdom of God. Just as the children of Israel *came out* of Egypt by faith in the work of God on their behalf, so we *come out* of our slavery to sin by faith in the work of Christ on our behalf. The Red Sea of His blood destroyed the works of the enemy in our lives, freeing us forever!

The wilderness is a place of preparation for entering the Promised Land. It is in the wilderness that God's people learn to live by faith in God's character and promises. *He provides for their every need*—food, water, imperishable clothing, no diseases, guidance and instruction in His ways. In the wilderness, they were *tested* so they would learn to trust God and His leader Moses. In the wilderness, they were *disciplined* for their unbelief, yet not cast aside as no longer God's people. Every believer in Christ enters a "wilderness of preparation" where we learn to live by faith in God and His promises. Jesus Christ is the "greater than Moses" Who gives us His law, is the true manna, water of life, light in the darkness, serpent on the pole, true tabernacle, ultimate sacrifice for sin, ultimate high priest, and the One who disciplines us and prepares us to enjoy our inheritance in Him.

The Promised Land does *not* represent Heaven but *the inheritance* of God's people. In the Promised Land, there are giants and wars. This is not true of Heaven. The only way out of the wilderness and into the Promised Land is by faith in God's character and promises. Our only way out of our wilderness and into the enjoyment of our inheritance in Christ is by faith in God's character and promises. It is through faith in Jesus Christ that we enter God's rest in our souls and learn to claim the inheritance we have in Him.

The "Egypt, Wilderness, Promised Land" paradigm enables us to see the five warning passages as motivators to faith, not threats to our salvation.

WARNINGS

Hebrews contains five of some the most severe warning passages in the New Testament, warnings that have caused many to fear losing their salvation. I am convinced these warning passages are true warnings to believers but that they do *not* contain a threat of losing one's salvation. They are intended to *instruct* us in God's grace and to demonstrate that God's *extravagant grace* always comes with His *extensive discipline*. The inspired author of Hebrews insists on playing God's grace melody with a three-part harmony; grace instructs us to *deny* ungodliness, to *live* righteously and to *hope* in the coming of Christ. The five warning passages of the book expose us to the grace that calls us to *deny* sin and *live* unto God.

The warning passages are progressively intensive and are part of God's three-part harmony of "grace instructions" to us. Just as God warned the children of Israel in the wilderness to live by faith in God's promises or face severe discipline, so He warns us to do the same (1 Corinthians 10:1–22). The wilderness "grace-warnings" were given to prepare God's people for claiming their inheritance in the Promised Land, not threats to send them back to Egypt and lose their salvation! God gives warnings to His redeemed people because His grace refuses to let them go. His grace is always extravagant, yet His discipline is always extensive. God's relentless "disciplining grace" is outlined in the five warning passages of Hebrews.

Drift (Hebrews 2:1–4)

"For this reason (because God has spoken fully and finally in Jesus Christ), we must pay much closer attention to what we have heard, so that we do not *drift away* from it." *We* are to pay attention to God's revelation to us in Christ because *God* is paying close attention to us! Lack of intentional listening leads to drifting away and hearing another voice. The drift is usually slow and subtle. We neglect God's Word, prayer, and fellowship with His people. We become more anxious, increasingly self-focused, and our relationships with God and people suffer. If we do not repent, the pace of our drift picks up speed and, we move to Stage Two.

Deception (Hebrews 3:7–4:13)

Today, if you hear His voice do not harden your heart . . . take care that there not be in any one of you an evil, unbelieving heart . . .

*so that none of you will be hardened by the **deceitfulness** of sin . . .
they were not able to enter (God's rest) because of unbelief . . . they
failed to enter (God's rest) because of **disobedience** . . . do not fall by
following the same example of **disobedience**.* (Emphasis mine.)

Rest is mentioned ten times in this warning passage and
refers to the internal rest of heart and mind that flows into the
life of one who believes God's promises. Disobedience to God's
Word is always accompanied by *deception*. Jesus said that His
disciples abide in His word and therefore know the truth and
are set free (John 8:31–32). The opposite is also true: If we
ignore God's Word, we will believe lies and live in bondage.
Disobedience blocks our ability to experience rest in our heart
and mind, deceives us, and puts us in bondage to anxiety, discouragement, and selfishness. If we do not repent, the downward spiral picks up momentum and we enter Stage Three
discipline.

Dull of Hearing (Hebrews 5:11–6:12).

*Concerning him we have much to say, and it is hard to explain
since you have become **dull of hearing** . . . you have come to need milk
and not solid food . . . in the case of those who have once been enlightened and have tasted the heavenly gift and have been made partakers of the Holy Spirit and have tasted the good word of God and the
power of the age to come and then have fallen away, **it is impossible
to renew them again to repentance** . . . but beloved we are convinced
of better things concerning you . . . so that you will be imitators of
those who faith and patience inherit the promises.* (Emphasis mine.)

Those who have drifted, been disobedient, and fallen into
deception are now dull of hearing. He did not say "dead of hearing," but "dull of hearing." He intentionally uses language to
describe the saved: "you have come to need milk, you were
enlightened, tasted the heavenly gift, been made partakers of
the Holy Spirit . . . and then fallen away. It is impossible to go

back and start over; you are in the family of God, and therefore you will face divine discipline." He uses the analogy of burning fruitless ground to purify the soil so it will be productive again. God's persevering grace is extensive in its discipline. If repentance does not occur, then Stage Four discipline will soon arrive.

Defiant (Hebrews 10:19–39)

*Therefore, brethren since we have confidence to enter the holy place . . . and since we have a great priest over the house of God let us draw near . . . let us hold fast the confession of our hope . . . let us consider how to stimulate one another to love and good deeds . . . **if we go on sinning willfully after receiving the knowledge of the truth**, there no longer remains a sacrifice for sins but a terrifying expectation of judgment . . . the Lord will judge His people . . . knowing that you have for yourselves a better possession and a lasting one . . . you have need of endurance . . .* (Emphasis mine.)

A believer who drifts, becomes disobedient, deceived, and dull of hearing will become defiant. Good things in their life become "god things," the conscience is violated, selfishness increases, and "taking control of one's own life" becomes dominant. Emptiness, misery, stress, and discontentment dominate the mind and soul. If repentance does not occur, then severe Stage Five discipline will.

Defiled (Hebrews 12:14–29).

*See to it that no one comes short of the grace of God; that no root of bitterness springing up causes trouble, and by it many be **defiled** . . . see to it that you **do not refuse Him who is speaking**. For if those did **not escape** when they refused him who warned them on earth, **much less will we escape** who turn away for Him who warns from heaven. And his voice shook the earth . . . yet once more I will shake not only the earth but the heaven . . . we have received a kingdom which cannot be shaken, let us show gratitude.* (Emphasis mine.)

God will severely discipline His defiled ones to break them and bring them back to repentance. There is a list I never want to be on: the list of those whom God opposes. "God is opposed to the proud but gives grace to the humble" (James 4:6).

The increasing intensity of God's "instructing grace" proves His unwavering commitment to mold us into the image of Jesus Christ. This has motivated me to cooperate with Him in minding the slow leaks in my life. I suggest you memorize them and share them with a friend.

Drift → Deceived → Dull of Hearing → Defiant → Defiled

What does grace-instructed leadership look like when you encounter sheep in your flock who have drifted into big ditches? As we discovered in Chapter Three, Jesus expects His church to love each other enough to confront sin and exercise restorative discipline. Grace-instructed leaders must lead the way and welcome that discipline in their own lives.

At the beginning of this chapter, I told you how my father administered grace to me when I was a wayward fifteen-year-old boy. Many years later, I was called on to show the same kind of grace, in a more structured and restorative way, to a congregant in the early years of my ministry. It was a baptism by fire.

Nina has given me permission to share her story. I first met her when I was a candidate at the church I now pastor. I was invited to spend a week getting to know the church family and had the opportunity to visit in many homes. Her story captured my heart.

She had cancer, and as a result, her marriage ended and she lost custody of her three children. She lacked family support, so the church was covering her rent, taking her to doctor appointments, and helping her with practical needs. This had been going on for three years. A few months later, when I was selected as the new pastor, one of the first things I did was organize teams of people to share the load in assisting Nina. I got to know her and stayed connected with her care team. This continued for another three years.

One Sunday morning after the worship service, Nina approached me with one of her friends. Nina was in a frantic state and insisted on meeting with me in my office. When the three of us sat down, Nina began to sob. Once she gained her composure, she said, "I am so ashamed and have a confession to make. I have never had cancer, and I have deceived you and this church and so many others for six years. Please forgive me!"

I was flabbergasted and began to ask her questions. During the years I had known her, she had gone to the length of shaving her head to make it appear that she was going through chemotherapy. Her long list of doctors and medications was completely fake. She was a master con and had built her identity on deception at the expense of our church family.

She answered all my questions and seemed genuinely broken over her deception. I began to pray and formulate a response. I told her that I did forgive her but clarified the difference between forgiveness and restoration of trust. I read scriptures to her and told her that she was about to begin a journey of restoration that would be long and hard. She declared that she would do whatever I and the church asked of her.

Our leaders mapped out a path forward for her. We decided not to prosecute her legally, but we did ask her to go through a season of discipline toward a path of restoration as a member of our church family. Our plan involved seven steps which we fully implemented over a period of two years.

First, I insisted on meeting with her and her three children so that she could tell them the truth and ask for their forgiveness. We also arranged for her children to receive counseling. Her children were shocked, but they did forgive her and benefited from the counseling they received.

Second, I asked her to come to a meeting with all her caregivers and have her tell them the truth and ask their forgiveness. She did. We explained to them our seven-step plan, and they all forgave her and agreed to be a part of the restoration, if needed.

Third, I asked her to repeat the process with our board. She held nothing back and expressed genuine sorrow over her deception. She answered their questions and agreed to submit to the plan we outlined. The board members forgave her and agreed to be a part of her restoration plan.

Fourth, we refused to give her any more money. We required her to find a job and begin to support herself.

Fifth, we asked her to do volunteer work at the church to make simple restitution for her deception over the years. We did this for her conscience's sake.

Sixth, we asked her to take part in extensive counseling, to be mentored by two godly women in the church, and to meet with me on a consistent basis.

Seventh, we asked her to come before the church family, tell them the truth, and ask for forgiveness. We explained the principle of private sin requiring a private rebuke and public sin requiring a public rebuke. She had publicly deceived the church family, and for her own sake and the good of the church, this needed to be processed in a way that would lead to her healing and theirs. We wanted to experience the grace of God ourselves and pass it on to her, but we wanted to do so in a way that restores and leads to being instructed by the grace of God.

We gathered the church family on Sunday evening, and I explained the biblical basis for church discipline and our call to restore those of our fellowship who fall. I explained the seven-step process we were following and invited Nina to come forward. She confessed her deception, expressed genuine repentance, and asked for their forgiveness with the realization that she would enter a process of restoration. One of the most beautiful sights I have ever seen is the entire church family standing to their feet to express their forgiveness and willingness to work with her as she began the process of restoration.

Over the next two years, Nina worked hard and kept the commitments we asked of her. At the end of two years, we planned a night of restoration. That Sunday evening, we heard testimonies from her boss, her creditors, her co-workers, her children, her mentors, and her counselors. They each gave good reports on her, and our church family officially restored her to full fellowship.

Nina continued to grow in Christ through the years, married one of her former caregivers, and now lives happily with her husband and children in another state. When I called her recently, she said, "That was one of the most loving things that has ever happened to me." Nina knows that God's grace is extravagant in its mercy but extensive in its discipline. In the context of a church family who "graced her," she learned that God's grace instructs us to *deny* ungodliness, to *live* righteously, and to *hope* in the coming of Christ.

LET'S END WHERE WE BEGAN.

Are you a grace-instructed leader?
Do you now know how to tell if you are?
Are you amazed by the grace of God?

Turn the truths about God's grace into a daily prayer. Right now, renew your commitment to be a grace-instructed leader by relying fully on God's amazing grace.

Heavenly Father, I know You want me to be a leader who thrives and finishes strong. I confess my unbelief in Your assuring grace and my resistance to Your extensive discipline. I repent and now fully surrender myself to You. Open my eyes to see and be amazed by Your grace. Empower me to immediately say no to sin, eagerly say yes to You, and faithfully hope in Your kingdom. Turn me into a leader who is passionate for Your glory and eager to join You in Your mission of grace every day of my life.

WORKOUTS TO THRIVE AND FINISH STRONG

Review the chapter and share its basic concepts with someone else. Work through the following questions to ensure you understand and are applying its core truths:

1. How are you currently letting the grace of God instruct you? Which of the three aspects (denying ungodliness, living righteously, hoping in the coming of Christ) do you find most difficult to ingrain into your daily life? Why? What is your plan to repent and renew your instruction in the grace of God?
2. What insights from the book of Hebrews did you find most helpful? Why?
3. Have you experienced the five stages of Hebrews warning passages? Which of the warnings do you find most motivating? Why?
4. Review The 32/18 Principle (see appendix) each day for a week until you can recall many of its

tenets by memory. Which ones motivate you the most? Why?

5. Work through the "Spare the Rod and Spoil the Church" worksheet (below). Identify five guiding principles regarding church discipline, and support your answers with Scripture.

Spare the Rod and Spoil the Church

Scripture	Problem	Process	Purposes
1 Corinthians 5:1–13			
2 Corinthians 2:5–11			
Matthew 18:15–20			
Luke 17:3–4			
Romans 16:17–20			
Galatians 2:11–14			
Galatians 6:1–5			
1 Thessalonians 5:14–15			
2 Thessalonians 3:6–15			
1 Timothy 5:19–21			
2 Timothy 2:23–26			
Titus 1:10–16			
Titus 3:9–11			
2 John 9–11			
3 John 9–10			

CHAPTER 5

Keep the Home Fires Burning

*One relationship determines the health of **all** our relationships.*

E very married ministry leader who wants to thrive and finish strong needs to face a reality about relational priorities:
If you want to qualify as a leader worth following, your
relationship with God *must* shape your relationship with your
spouse. If this is not consistently evident to those who follow
you, then you are not qualified to lead God's people.

This sounds blunt and may be hard to swallow, so don't
take my word for it.

Paul insisted that leaders in a local church *first* demonstrate
a "one-woman kind of man" or "one-man kind of woman" heart
before assuming ministry leadership (1 Timothy 3:2, 12; Titus
1:6). Your faithful devotion to your spouse *is sourced in* your
faithful devotion to God. Being a "one-*God* kind of man or

woman" is revealed in being a "one-man" or "one-woman" kind of leader. If this is the standard for local church leaders, shouldn't it also be for leaders of other ministries who seek to honor Jesus Christ?

Why would Paul insist on this standard? Because marriage is so sacred that it reflects the oneness of the Trinity, displays the Gospel, and is one of God's chief tools to mold you into the image of Christ (Ephesians 5:28–33, Colossians 3:18–19). Learning to love, serve, and lead the mate God gave you equips you to love, serve, and lead the bride of Christ.

A godly leader who seems to be thriving everywhere but in his marriage recently asked me, "Why is it that I can get along so well with my co-workers, friends, relatives, and fellow believers but often find myself at odds with and irritated by my wife?"

I had listened to his story and knew him and his wife well, so I responded, "Because you are *one* with your wife and she knows you better than all the other people in your life. Therefore, God is using her to shine the spotlight on the areas of your character He wants to transform. He is calling you to submit to His refining work. This means death to having things your way and learning to submit to the Holy Spirit."

He agreed and is embracing the reality for him as a married leader: Thriving in ministry begins with his marriage.

Consider the generational impact of those who turn this reality into a conviction. My maternal grandparents were married seventy-one years. Their long-forged oneness has awed generations. Like the two Giant Sequoias that merged in Yosemite National Park, they too earned the title "The Faithful Couple."[1] I doubt if either my grandmother or grandfather ever read a marriage book other than God's master manual, the Bible. Yet their "marriage-rekindling teaching" by example and word has spread like a healing flame into the hearths of countless cold homes. Seven decades of hospitality, service and counseling flowed from their marriage bond. Much of what I have learned about "how to keep the home fires burning"[2] came from their influence and that of my own parents, who adored each other for forty-six years until they, too, were parted by death.

Their influence, along with four decades of studying and applying the Scriptures to my own marriage, has been used by God to deposit in me life-giving insights on how to keep the home fires burning. By God's grace (not just a cliché but a core conviction), I have invested more than forty years counseling couples working through marital conflicts, conducted more than four hundred weddings, and have been happily married to my sweetheart, Mae Belle, for forty-five years.

Some of the core insights that have sustained my own marriage and hundreds of others are contained in this chapter. Keeping the home fires burning is one of the *essentials* for leaders to thrive and finish strong.

FACE THE BAD NEWS, FEED YOUR FAITH ON THE GOOD NEWS

All marriages naturally drift toward isolation because we are selfish and sinful. Marriages do not fail because of blowouts; they fail because of many unattended slow leaks. As a leader, read those two sentences again and consider their implications. Beware the slow leaks in your marriage.

Good news! God's cure will stop the drift, steer couples into the harbor of marital intimacy, and repair the leaks. I have

experienced the power of His timeless truths in my own marriage and have seen them restore hundreds of seemingly hope-
less unions.

Fourteen years ago, I was stopped in my tracks by a story
from a strong ministry leader. He had been leading a flourishing church in Queens, New York, for nearly a decade. He was
forced to face the reality that God was intentionally using his
marriage to make him face deep-seated issues that were about
to sabotage his life and ministry.

One day when he came home, his wife greeted him with
that look that said, "We need to talk." She lovingly and calmly
told him she was quitting the church because of his packed
schedule, people-pleasing habits, and refusal to face some hard
realities. She even said she would be happier separated from him
than living with him. This forced them both to seek help. Their
journey resulted in a restored marriage, a healthy ministry, and
keen biblical insights on emotionally healthy marriage and
ministry leadership.

Their marriage crisis could have resulted in devastation for
them, their children, and hundreds of other married leaders in
their church. Instead, their repentance and renewal has been used
by God to restore countless marriage that have been blown off
course and ministry leaders who have gotten out of alignment. His
story and resulting insights have served as a wake-up call to me.[3]

Never underestimate the ripple effect your marriage will
have on so many others, either for God's glory or Satan's delight
(John 10:10). Face the fact that the story of your marriage is tied
to God's story; one should reinforce the other.

**Your marriage cannot be properly understood without
connecting it to the story line of the Bible.**

It is fascinating to realize that the Bible opens and closes with a marriage: the union of Adam and Eve and the marriage supper of the Lamb (Genesis 2:18–25; Revelation 19:7–10, 21:2). In the middle, God is portrayed as a lover who is in pursuit of an intimate, fully committed love relationship with us (Isaiah 54:6–8, Luke 19:10).

The Bible consistently uses marital imagery to portray the union God wants to enjoy with us.

- He declares to Israel that "the Lord is your husband" and rebukes her for acting like an unfaithful harlot (Isaiah 54:5, Jeremiah 3:20, Hosea 2:2)
- Jesus is called "the bridegroom" and performed His first miracle at a wedding in Cana (John 2:1–11).
- At the Last Supper, Jesus, with the broken bread and poured-out wine, is essentially saying, "This is the price I am willing to pay to win my bride."
- Paul quotes God's definition of marriage from Genesis 2 and then declares he is speaking of Christ and the church (Ephesians 5:31–32).
- Paul is thus proclaiming that *every* marriage is a signpost which points to the ultimate marriage God longs for us to experience in Jesus Christ. No wonder the author of Hebrews insists that marriage is to be held in honor among all and its bed left undefiled (Hebrews 13:4).

As a ministry leader, have you intentionally connected the story of your marriage to God's story? Do you realize you are either proclaiming His story or perverting it by how you function in your marriage?

**Effectively proclaiming God's story demands that we
develop a covenant mindset in our marriage.**

Normal people do not consider getting rid of their children
because they are not meeting their needs—but it's amazing how
many believers, let alone society in general, display a willingness
to divorce their spouse for that reason.

Ask any parent if their child has cost them money, time,
and sacrifice, and the answer will always be yes. Probe further
by asking, "Does your child try your patience, show a lack of
respect at times, and not appreciate your sacrifices for them?"
Again, the answer will be yes. But ask the same parent if they
have seriously considered divorcing their children or giving
them away, and the answer will be an emphatic no! When it
comes to our children, we have a covenant mindset—and the
Bible tells us we need to have that same kind of approach to
our marriages.

Just as a healthy parent does not ignore selfishness and sin
in their child, so we do not ignore selfishness and sin in our
marriage relationships. However, sin and selfishness must first
be confronted in our *own* hearts, and only then are we equipped
to help our mates overcome their faults (Galatians 6:1–2). None
of us marry a perfectly fulfilling soulmate, but we can be linked
to God, the only One who can ultimately fulfill us.

We are going to unpack how to cultivate the covenant
mindset in marriage in some ways you may have never considered. It begins by facing an underlying truth that is often ignored.

Being married to Mae Belle is one of the greatest delights
of my life. We are each other's best friend and safe place. The
reason our marriage is satisfying, though, is not because we are
great people or because we just happened to find the perfect
soulmate. We are different in many ways and are both sinners

who habitually work through hurts, conflicts, and disappointments. *The foundational reason* that we are enjoying a healthy marriage is because we believe a truth that keeps on setting us free:

One relationship determines the health of *all* our relationships.

The one relationship is with God, who created us in His image and designed marriage for our good and His glory.

Mae Belle is a teacher of humanities and writing to seventh and eighth graders at Rivendell Christian School. Her belief in our conviction is reflected on a large banner she hung across the front of her classroom. It reads *Soli Deo Gloria*: "to God alone be the glory." This is our North Star and motivation in marriage. It undergirds our conviction that one relationship determines the health of all our relationships.

Does this mean that unbelievers cannot have a healthy marriage? Absolutely not! Marriage was designed by God for the whole human race. It is a gift of His common grace. Thus, marriages between unbelievers who align with His design can also enjoy the benefits that come from that alignment. However, when the Lord is the center and foundation of a marriage, it moves to a new level of intimacy and opens doors to a power that cannot be obtained any other way.

How does the "one relationship" with God spill over into our marriage relationship?

Mae Belle and I began our married life in Portland, Oregon. A delightful place we discovered on the coast serves as a parable that has helped us and many others develop a healthy marriage: Depot Bay, whose entrance sign boasts that it's "the world's smallest harbor." The quaintness and beauty of the town captured us, and I was fascinated by alluring advertisements to go deep-sea fishing. When our oldest son turned four, I took him to Depot Bay to enjoy a father-son outing before our family moved to Virginia.

Our deep-sea fishing adventure has been etched into our memories ever since. Our boat captain delighted us by trolling alongside whales, and he rewarded our investment with a catch of several large salmon each. As the sun was setting, we made our way back to the entrance of the "world's smallest harbor." The captain stopped the boat and called all the passengers to the front of his craft. His stern tone captured our attention, and his observations of our surroundings struck fear in our hearts. He noted the coming storm on the horizon, the churning cross currents in front of the rock-lined harbor we were about to enter, and the crashed boat on the sharp rocks near us. He brought to our attention several buoys in the water in front of the harbor's narrow entrance. He explained that he would have to steer the boat so that the buoys were so perfectly aligned that they would appear as one. His lecture was almost an appeal for prayer as he explained that we would not make it in safely if he failed to properly align the watercraft with the buoys. The good news is that he did, and I came away with a marriage-mending parable.

Every couple begins their marriage hoping to enter the safe harbor of marital intimacy after they sail the seas of life together. They enjoy whale-like delights and pulling into their new home treasures they have caught along the way. But when the stresses of life, inevitable relational conflicts, and countless distractions blow them off course, they do not always look to the Ultimate Captain of every marriage for help. Many ignore His warnings and wise directives and crash on the shore outside the secure harbor of marital intimacy.

However, there is hope, even for those who have crashed on the sharp rocks. Shipwrecked and damaged marriages can be restored. There is also hope for those who are blown off course and headed for the rocks. Submitting to the Ultimate Marriage Captain's plan leads directly into the harbor of safety and intimacy.

God has placed five essential buoys of truth before the entrance to the harbor of marital health. If we learn to make wise choices in alignment with His directives, we are on the way to enjoying marriage as He intended. Genesis 2:18–25 records *God's definition of marriage*[4] and the five relational choices that lead into the harbor of marital intimacy.

Let's discover how to invite into our marriage the One Who designed it. These five choices are indispensable for married ministry leaders to master and model! Remember that your marriage puts the Gospel on display, and effective leadership for a married ministry leader begins at home.

FIVE RELATIONAL CHOICES THAT LEAD TO MARITAL INTIMACY

Then the LORD God said, "It is not good for the man to be alone; I will make him a helper suitable for him." Out of the ground the LORD God formed every beast of the field and every bird of the sky, and brought them to the man to see what he would call them; and whatever the man called a living creature, that was its name. The man gave names to all the cattle, and to the birds of the sky, and to every beast of the field, but for Adam there was not found a helper suitable for him. So the LORD God caused a deep sleep to fall upon the man, and he slept; then He took one of his ribs and closed up the flesh at that place. The LORD God fashioned into a woman the rib which He had taken from the man and brought her to the man. The man said,

> *"This is now bone of my bones,*
> *And flesh of my flesh;*
> *She shall be called Woman,*
> *Because she was taken out of Man."*

For this reason a man shall leave his father and his mother and be joined to his wife; and they shall become one flesh. And the man and his wife were both naked and were not ashamed (Genesis 2:18-25).

A "safe-harbor" marriage is one that is oriented around what God says marriage is:

One man and one woman in a covenant relationship built around five wise choices in which they commit their whole person to each other for life.

CHOICE ONE: SEE YOUR MATE AS A GIFT FROM GOD

The man said, "This is now bone of my bones, and flesh of my flesh; She shall be called Woman, because she was taken out of Man." (Genesis 2:23)

God performed the first operation in history, designed a woman for Adam, and brought her to him. When Adam woke up from his "surgery" in the recovery room, he was delightfully surprised by what God made from his rib. Adam broke into poetry-praise and set the tone that millions have echoed throughout history and Etta James captured in her song "At Last!" He received her as a gift from God, and she reciprocated in a one-flesh relationship.

Before Eve, Adam lived in the ultimate awe-inspiring environment with fascinating things to explore, yet there was no one corresponding to him. God designed Adam and Eve for each other and established their marriage as a pattern for all who would follow them. Their first step toward intimacy was receiving each other as a gift from God. This is also the first step for all who long to enter the harbor of marital intimacy.

Married ministry leaders create a sense of security and stability among those they lead when they model receiving your mate as a gift from God. People from broken families love seeing unity, honor, and gratitude modeled in the marriage of their leader. It gives them hope. Demonstrating a "one-woman kind of man" or "one-man kind of woman" character creates safety among team members. Receiving your mate as a gift from God also fosters a healthy spiritual environment built on gratitude.

Marriage is about oneness and is designed to refine our character. I often tell couples, "Do you realize that the primary person God wants to use to refine your character and make you like Christ is sitting next to you? If you do not value their differences, you are robbing yourself and dishonoring them and the God who brought you together. If you cultivate the habit of valuing your differences, you will grow in wisdom, experience true intimacy, and glorify God."

Helping each other become like Christ should be the filter through which we view our marriages. It causes us to see our partners' differences as hidden treasures we need instead of irritants we would rather live without. Because we are partnering in union with God, our differences need to be respected, not trashed. Our response to our mate's differences will either move us closer to the harbor of intimacy or push us near the rocks of isolation. Couples often begin delighting in each other and enjoying the ways they differ, but when conflicts arise, they are tempted to "return to sender."

One of our first major conflicts was over purchasing our first sofa. I was in my last year of seminary and had just started in my role as a new pastor. Our budget was extremely tight, and we were committed to graduating from seminary debt-free. Mae's grandmother sent us money to purchase our first new piece of furniture.

My approach to shopping was to decide what we wanted, go find the best product, buy it, and move on. Much like a hunter, my motto was "Kill it, bag it, and take it home!" Mae Belle is a wise planner and prudent shopper. We stepped into the furniture store and surveyed what seemed to me to be dozens of sofa options. We finally discovered a sofa that appeared to be perfect for our needs. The salesman was helpful and eager to answer all of Mae's questions. She wanted to know where the sofa was made, where the fabric came from, the warranty, and many other questions. The salesman was a talker and from my point of view needed to "bottom-line it." I was rude and impatient and clearly demonstrated my desire to make the purchase and move on.

We eventually purchased the sofa of our choice, but as we walked out of the store, Mae Belle said, "I hope that salesman never finds out you are a pastor!" I failed the "value your mate's differences" test that day, but her rebuke convicted me and moved me in the right direction.

When we began our marriage, I lacked confidence in academics while Mae Belle was a Phi Beta Kappa scholar. On the other hand, she lacked confidence in social settings while I could easily relate to anyone. Over the years, she has boosted my confidence and helped me hone my academic skills; now she is sought out as a wise counselor, and most people who know her consider her one of their best friends. The changes in both of us can be traced to learning to accept each other as a gift from God.

Embracing the truth that we are each a gift from God to each other has set us free from ever believing the lie that we married the wrong person. Perseverance and learning to adjust forge emotional bonds that can lead to a happy marriage. Did you know that two-thirds of the couples in trouble who stay together five years end up reconciled?[5]

One practical way to apply the principle of receiving your mate as a gift from God is to make it a habit to encourage him or her. Memorize Ephesians 4:29 together and practice applying it on each other: "Let no unwholesome word proceed from your mouth, but only such a word as is good for edification according to the need of the moment, so that it will give grace to those who hear."

Mae Belle gave me a small rock many years ago, and it sits in the center of the table in my office. She wrote on it in dark permanent ink, "You are my hero." Countless times, I have glanced at that rock and thanked God for my gift, who is very *different* from me.

CHOICE TWO: LEAVE YOUR FATHER AND MOTHER

For this reason, a man shall leave his father and his mother and be joined to his wife; and they shall become one flesh. (Genesis 2:24)

Learning to leave father and mother is an essential step toward becoming a godly leader. It requires faith in God, maturity to stand on your own, and the skill to honor your parents while growing in independence. Doing it well demonstrates maturity to those you lead.

Learning to leave father and mother includes facing the influence of unhealthy models and learning to let Jesus Christ and His Word shape your marriage. This was part of my leaving process.

My father was a godly man, an excellent husband, and in many ways, my hero. However, his father died when my dad was only nine. His mother grew bitter over her husband's death and chose her daughter as her favorite. This caused my dad to become strongly independent and somewhat controlling. I soon realized that I brought many of those same traits into my own marriage, and it dishonored and wounded Mae Belle. I had to face this and be intentional about leading like Jesus and not like what was modeled to me.

Did you notice the verse begins with "for this reason"? The phrase pushes us back to Adam's declaration that Eve was bone of his bones and flesh of his flesh. In other words, they were of the same source and designed for oneness. For this reason, because marriage is about oneness, a man shall leave his father and mother. Both husband and wife are to leave father and mother. The leaving is a deliberate choice, and if it not done properly, couples will not enter the harbor of marital intimacy. Leaving father and mother does not mean to abandon your responsibility to them, but it does mean that you shift your primary allegiance from them to your marriage partner. It means to break the dependent, child-parent bond and replace it with a healthy allegiance to your marriage.

Notice that God's instruction to leave father and mother was not limited to Adam and Eve. Neither of them had a physical father and mother. Therefore, these instructions are for all marriages. That is one of the reasons this passage is quoted through the Old Testament and into the New. Genesis 2 provides a pattern that all marriages are to cut along.

It may surprise you to learn that you will not be able to effectively cleave unto your mate if you refuse to leave your father and mother. In marriage, leaving *precedes* cleaving.

This is one of the reasons we must learn to obey the command to honor our father and our mother. If we learn to honor our parents, then we are protecting our marriage and moving it toward the harbor of intimacy. Never believe the lie that you can skip this step in the five wise choices God gives us for healthy marriages. All the choices are essential, and to skip one is like trying to walk with only one leg.

Healthy ministry leaders honor their father and mother. If they don't, they will discover the boat there are seeking to captain is leaking! As a leader, determine to obey the command to honor your father and mother. Otherwise, it will impact your relationship with God, your ability to relate to those in authority, and how you use your authority. Make it a priority to ensure that all those on your team are honoring their fathers and mothers. Ignore this, and it will come back and bite you and those you lead.

In the early days of my twenty-nine years with a global mission agency, I discovered the biggest problem missionaries have in the field is not with language, adjusting to the culture, raising support, or communicating effectively with unbelievers: It's that missionaries cannot get along with each other. And many of the conflicts can be traced to a broken relationship with parents

Andera, a natural leader, was a gifted and godly young woman in our missionary training program. In the process of mentoring her, we discovered that she "hated" her father. We insisted that she work through the issues and do all she could to reconcile with him before we sent her to the field. She labored over the process, but God honored her efforts, and she and her father were wonderfully reconciled.

Six months after arriving on the field, her father suddenly died. She immediately called us and thanked us profusely for insisting that she reconcile with her father. She said with tears of joy, "I have no regrets." Today she is a grandmother, and she and her husband are experiencing the joy of seeing generations walk in the ways of God!

In our premarital mentoring ministry, we intentionally help couples learn to honor their father and mother for the sake of their marriage and the glory of God. We ask them to write a tribute to their parents and present it in a private setting before the wedding. A resource that will help you wisely put a tribute together is available online.[6]

In the first year of our marriage, Mae Belle flew from Oregon to Georgia to clear her conscience and do all she could to reconcile with her father. Her mother is a godly woman, but her father was the exact opposite. He left a trail of hurt and pain in the hearts of all six of his children. Mae Belle had witnessed his negative influence on her mother and her siblings, but she had been a good daughter and had honored her father the best she knew how. However, a seed of bitterness began to take root in her heart. God honored her trip home not only to release her from resentment but to bless her mother and siblings. It enabled her to "leave" and more effectively cleave to me. Our sons benefited many times over because she broke the chain of bitterness.

Cleaving to our mate means we must grow up and intentionally let go of our "childish ways." Children are dependent and do not plan. We must learn to be independent from parents, one with our mate, and decide in advance with our spouse how we will handle a host of challenges. Decide together how you will handle uninvited advice and other boundary breakers.

Children can be tattletales, but mature marriage partners refuse to give bad reports on their parents or in-laws.

Determine to align the boat of your marriage with the buoy of leaving father and mother—it is an essential for entering the harbor of marital intimacy.

CHOICE THREE: CLEAVE UNTO YOUR MATE

For this reason, a man shall leave his father and his mother and be joined to his wife; and they shall become one flesh. (Genesis 2:24)

As a married ministry leader, you are called to model losing your life to find it (Matthew 10:39). Have you considered how your marriage is a primary context to demonstrate this quality to those whom you lead?

"To cleave" literally means "to be glued together." This is the basis of our "till death do we part" vow. Seal up the back door to your marriage, and do not leave any cracks! Marriage is sacred, and its oneness reflects the oneness of the Trinity. Cleaving to your mate means to refuse to pour acids on the glue of your covenant vow. Never threaten divorce; instead commit to put super glue on your union and turn conflicts into opportunities to renew your allegiance to each other.

Once, when Mae Belle and I were speaking at a marriage conference, she shared how this principle changed her thinking early on.

"The first major fight we had occurred in the first month of our marriage," she said. "We had just moved to Oregon, and I literally did not know anyone except for my husband. As the intensity of disagreement mounted, I walked out of our apartment and hopped on the first city bus I saw, not knowing where on earth I was going. As I rode around Portland for hours, the reality of my situation dawned on me: *You can't go home to your mom, you do not know anyone here to whom you can go and complain, and it is getting dark!* There was a seismic shift in my thinking at that point: *Mae, your first allegiance from now on is to your husband. He is your refuge; cleave to him. Go home and work this out."*

The biblical patterns of allegiance involve respect (following) for the wife and sacrificial love (leadership) for the husband. Ephesians 5 makes this crystal clear.

"My allegiance, my cleaving, to Steve is show in my supporting his efforts all the way from picking out a new car to his plans to counsel one of our sons to his decisions about our church," Mae Belle said. "I deeply value all my husband does in our marriage, and I have grown to appreciate how much I really need him. But we do not always see eye-to-eye. That is where I must check my heart; is my trust really in God who can work in, through, around, and over my husband?"

The Scriptures tell me that one of my roles as a godly husband is leadership. This means I am to lovingly serve Mae by taking the responsibility to provide for her and protect her. I protect her by serving her so that she does not go over the cliff of being overwhelmed. I also protect her by speaking God's truth in love to her in the context of understanding listening. I protect her by being committed to sexual purity—guarding my eyes and being a one-woman kind of man. This makes it possible for her heart to be at rest.

Cleaving, for both husband and wife, means protecting each other's reputation. When you share details about your marriage, always check your motives. Does the person need to hear because they are part of the solution, or is it just a bad report? A bad report is sharing negative information about another with someone who is not part of the solution and does not need to know the information.

Cleaving also means courageously cleaning out the acids that eat away at the bond of your marriage. Call sin what it is and repent—stop making excuses and be intentional about keeping your sacred bond. The acid of preoccupation with work or projects is neglect. The acid of pornography and unfaithful fantasies are breaking your vows. The acid of self-justification is prideful and feeds bitterness.

Cleaving means to love each other faithfully. We need to learn to love by faith and not just feelings. Feelings come and go, but your faith in Christ can last and grow. Your faith is no better than its object; if you choose the risen Jesus Christ, He will infuse you with His love. Romans 5:5 says, "The love of God has been poured out within the heart of a believer."

In the early years of our marriage, we attended a conference where we learned the concept of loving by faith. God's love is in us by the Holy Spirit, Who loves our mate perfectly 24/7, 365. We must claim this love by faith, especially when we don't feel love. After the conference, we had a disagreement driving home and ended up driving around the perimeter of our city five times seeking to resolve our differences. When we finally arrived home that evening, I asked Mae Belle, "Do you love me?" She responded, "By faith!" That is the point. She did not feel love at the time, but she could claim God's love by faith and join Him in loving me.

Many believe being "in love" is a feeling and when that feeling disappears, perhaps it's time to move on. But that is completely backwards: Your love will not sustain your covenant; your covenant *will* sustain your love.

The key to staying married is not staying in a state of emotional love but keeping the covenant promises you make before God and practicing true love that goes beyond emotions to actions. The Bible's famous "love" chapter, 1 Corinthians 13, uses sixteen adjectives to describe love—and not one of them is a feeling. Every single one of them represents a byproduct of faith in Jesus Christ. Love is a volitional act of the will that moves to a new level when we bask in the love God has extended to us through His Son Jesus Christ. Our committed love in marriage will be an illustration of His grace. Remember that Jesus keeps His "super-glue" vow to you even when you fail—He said, "I am with you always, even to the end of the world!" (Matthew 28:20) Let His commitment to you shape your commitment to cleave unto your mate.

CHOICE FOUR: BECOME ONE FLESH

For this reason, a man shall leave his father and his mother and be joined to his wife; and they shall become one flesh (Genesis 2:24).

As a leader, make becoming one flesh with your mate a top priority. This glorifies God, helps you resists temptation, models commitment, produces healthy personal growth, encourages your mate, breeds security in your children, and will satisfy you.

God's intention is that both marriage partners experience the positive and life-giving joy of becoming one flesh. The order of the wise choices is progressive: receive your mate as a gift from God, leave father and mother, cleave unto your mate, *then* become one flesh. The receiving, leaving, and cleaving create an environment to fully bond and begin the adventure of *becoming together.*

Picture a triangle with God at the top and husband and wife on each of the bases. As the husband and wife move up the base toward God, they also move closer to each other. When God is the focal point of marriage, His love and grace bring oneness. One relationship with Him shapes the marital relationship with each other.

My parents were constantly affectionate and appropriately modeled the beauty of delight in each other. At dinner, my brothers and I often heard Dad say, "Sons, if you end up marrying a woman half as good as your mom, you will have knocked it out of the park!" Dad would often do a little dance and snap his fingers as he sang "Ain't No Woman Like the One I've Got" by the Four Tops. All five of us King kids to this day delight in the sense of love and security our parents' romance gave us. That's leadership.

Leaders who make becoming one flesh with their marriage partner a priority also need to develop a healthy and robust theology of sex. Know well God's purposes for creating this gift, and teach it to those you lead. In our very confused culture, this is more important than ever.

Many assume there are only two basic perspectives when it comes to sexuality: the permissive view and the prudish view. The permissive view dominates our culture. It declares that sex is a natural appetite that one should be free to express if it does not harm others, and it supports building identity around one's sexual orientation. The prudish view is incorrectly assumed by many to be the biblical or traditional perspective. It declares that sex is a necessary appetite for procreation but is shameful and is to be tightly regulated.

The Bible's perspective does not align with either the permissive or prudish view. It teaches that God created sex for four positive purposes, all of which are linked to becoming one flesh. For ease of memorization, each purpose here begins with the letter P.

Portrayal of God's holy love. The three persons of the Trinity— God the Father, Son, and Holy Spirit—have eternally and perfectly loved and served each other, yet they are one. Men and women are created in the image of a triune God, and in the union of marriage, they portray the love and oneness of the Trinity (Genesis 1:26–28).

Paul made an astounding statement in Ephesians 5:31–32: *"For this reason a man shall leave his father and mother and shall be joined to his wife, and the two shall become one flesh.* This mystery is great; but I am speaking with reference to Christ and the church." He quotes the essential definition of marriage from Genesis 2:24 and then says he is referring to Christ and the church. In other words, all marriages between a man and a woman are intended to serve as signposts which point to Christ, where we will find ultimate love. Therefore, the sexual union is sacred and reserved for a whole-person commitment of self-giving love in the context of marriage. Only in this context can a couple become one flesh.

Permanence. There is a progressive mutuality embedded in the choices that lead to becoming one flesh. It is always preceded by receiving our mate as a gift from God, leaving father and mother, and cleaving to each other. The first three choices make the fourth possible.

Becoming one flesh includes union on all levels and is a life-long process. This is the basis of the marriage vows, which express an exclusive and progressively intimate commitment to another person till death do we part. Therefore, sex in marriage is a renewal of your "becoming one flesh" covenant vows. It is acting out the reality of your exclusive "one-woman kind of man and one-man kind of woman" union. No wonder the New Testament commands husband and wife to habitually "renew their vows" this way (1 Corinthians 7:1–5)!

Pleasure. Sexual pleasure, in the context of a "becoming one flesh" marriage, is built on mutual love and service to each other.

In marriage, our only options are being a servant or a manipulator, and often the bedroom reveals which we really are. Older marriage vows unite service and sex with six simple words: "With my body, I thee worship." The context of whole-person, exclusive, life-long, mutual service to each other maximizes sexual pleasure and glorifies God.

I was surprised to discover that our bodies are mentioned eight times in 1 Corinthians 6–7, and the command to glorify God with our bodies is in the context of sexual relationships (1 Corinthians 6:13–7:7). The first nine chapters of Proverbs are wise instructions given from a father to his son. It is interesting that five chapters are devoted to sex education with the clear teaching that, outside the covenant of marriage, sex is destructive but that, inside the marriage union, the pleasure is maximized. Consider Proverbs 5:18–19: "Let your fountain be blessed and rejoice in the wife of your youth. As a loving hind and a graceful doe, Let her breasts satisfy you at all times; Be exhilarated always with her love."

Procreation. God's first command to Adam and Eve was to be fruitful and multiply (Genesis 1:28), and Psalm 127:3–5 declares that children are a gift from God and the fruit of the womb is a reward. The ideal context for raising children is in a home where Mom and Dad are modeling a "one-flesh" relationship. One-flesh marriages bring joy and security to children and build a stable society.

Choice five: Transparency

And the man and his wife were both naked and were not ashamed (Genesis 2:25).

Transparency is a byproduct of internal security. When a ministry leader finds his or her security in Christ, then he or she is more prone to be transparent with his or her spouse. Fear of rejection or pride that prevents accountability is evidence of not being securely rooted in Christ.

Transparency is the jewel in the crown of the five wise choices. It is the payoff of making the first four choices, and this one transforms the others to a deeper level. It represents the kind of knowing and being known we all long for but are threatened by. The Hebrew word for "naked" literally means "laid bare." So this choice involves the most risk—baring our naked souls and revealing the shameful secrets in our hearts.

It is important to know that this fifth choice of transparency is not about pushing your marital relationship into a place it is not ready to go. If "laid bare" transparency makes you want to run—if being vulnerable before your mate seems like a set-up for manipulation, misunderstanding, disappointment, and hurt—then stay with me. I am going to share with you some insights which have proven to be effective in my own marriage and in hundreds of others over forty years of counseling.

Don't let your fears, past hurts, or negative assumptions rob you of the joy of venturing into the harbor of marital transparency! The good news is that we are not left to venture into this relational minefield alone and unprotected. The One Who designed marriage and created you and your mate has your back and is eager to guide you through the process.

The fifth choice is about nurturing a transparent relationship with God, Who will in turn shepherd you into experiencing transparency in your marriage.

One relationship determines the health of *all* our relationships.

Instead of focusing on the complicated nuances of learning how to be effectively transparent with each other, we have learned to focus on two simple disciplines in our walk with God. When we practice these two uncomplicated ways of connecting with God, He wisely and faithfully leads us into the harbor of marital intimacy.

Confession

Unhealthy ministry leaders have a hard time admitting they are wrong. Marriage provides a safe place to learn to do so and to get over our pride.

Memorize and embrace the 1 Timothy 1:15 mindset: "It is a trustworthy statement, deserving full acceptance, that Christ Jesus came into the world to save sinners, among whom *I am foremost of all.*" Do you honestly see yourself as the chief sinner in your marriage? If not, you may have a "log in the eye" problem that you need to repent of (Matthew 7:3–5). This does not mean we overlook abuse and extreme selfishness, but it does mean we don't overplay our mate's sins and downplay our own.

Twenty words often fall from the lips of those who confess their sins and enjoy transparency in marriage: *"I was wrong. It was my fault. I am sorry. Please forgive me. I love you."* Just as we daily brush our teeth and take out the trash, we need to habitually repent and neutralize the acids that erode our bond.

Humble leaders confess their sins, make things right, and live in the grace of transparency with God. Proud leaders refuse to confess and repent, and God opposes them (James 4:6). God opposes the proud and gives grace to the humble and so does our marriage partner! Confession and repentance simply mean you admit you were wrong and make things right. This is the key that opens the door to God's heart and transparency in marriage.

You will be motivated to confess your sins to God and make things right with others if you remember that God is like a lover who is pursuing you and wants to demonstrate His loyal love to you. Jesus Christ shed his blood to purchase you as His beloved. We can be absolutely assured that when we confess our sins to Him, we are fully forgiven.

Let me suggest the following three verses to memorize. They are designed to assure you that you are forgiven, cleansed, and accepted when you lay your soul bare to God.

- *If we confess our sins, he is faithful and righteous to forgive our sins and cleanse us from all unrighteousness.* (1 John 1:9)
- *By one sacrifice* (the death of Christ on the cross for us) *he has perfected forever those who are sanctified* (set apart in Christ as His child). (Hebrews 10:14)
- *There is no condemnation for those who are in Christ Jesus.* (Romans 8:1)

The habit of coming clean before God and experiencing His forgiveness will spill over into coming clean with our marriage partner. Transparency with God leads to transparency in our marriage. And transparency in our marriage helps us to become leaders who model it.

Prayer

Thriving ministry leaders habitually pray with their life partners. Find a pattern that fits your personalities. Some like to have set schedules to pray together, and others make it a natural flow in their lives.

Mae Belle and I go on a walk together almost every day, and during that time, we pray. We never go to sleep at night without praying together. We pray as we drive around, talk on the phone, and spontaneously pray around the house. The issue is not how long we pray but that we make it a habit. Our relationship began with prayer; we prayed on our first date, and praying together has motivated us to "keep short accounts" and led us into many adventures with God.

Six months before we married and moved across the country, we made a specific prayer list. It covered many things, including finding jobs, a place to live, and a new church home. An illustration of our specificity related to finding an apartment. We asked God to lead us to a place near the seminary for less than $100 dollars per month (this was 1973, and that wasn't unreasonable back then). We prayed that it would be furnished (since we had no furniture), have a fireplace, a bay window, a study, and a front porch.

We arrived in Portland and spent the day eagerly surveying rental ads and found nothing in line with our request. When we looked again the next day, Mae pointed out one that simply read, "Apartment $89 per month." I said, "That has to be a rat trap!" Mae responded, "We have been praying—let's take a look."

We drove a few blocks and discovered the apartment was near the seminary and on the edge of a beautiful old tree-lined street with rose gardens at each end. The apartment was part of a large fourplex and had a huge front porch. We opened the door to discover a fully furnished apartment with a fireplace, bay window, and study! We moved in that night, stayed there five years, and the rent never went up! This was a special grace gift from our heavenly Father, and it greatly encouraged us. It became a story we passed to our sons and now granddaughter.

Remember that there are three persons in your marriage—you, your mate, and God. Our normal inclination is to forget that God is part of the marriage. When you find your hope and security in Christ and remember He is the third person in the marriage, you can let go of the pattern of controlling and manipulating your mate out of selfishness and fear to get your needs met. Going to Jesus by faith and living out who you are in Him gives you the power and motivation to serve your mate from the heart.

Mae Belle shared at a conference how remembering God is the third person in our marriage has helped her countless times in living with me!

"On one occasion, my husband and I were talking over a difficult situation we faced. I felt very strongly that he ought to take a certain course of action, and although we talked for hours, way into the night, as I laid out my case as persuasively as I could, he said he just did not see the necessity for doing what I asked him to do. Well, I knew that to keep on and on about it would be counterproductive because trying to control some-one is certainly not ministering to them or serving them, but the next morning when I woke up, I felt a profound sense of loss and frustration. And then I remembered that there were three persons in our marriage—and although the dialogue on this issue was over between my husband and me, the conversation could continue between me and God.

"I began to pray, 'Lord, if this burden that I have is truly from You, work in my husband's heart so that he can embrace this perspective. Lord, You can change his thinking through people he meets, through insights he might hear on the radio, through a thousand different avenues. You can remold his thoughts. And if my plan is not what You ultimately want to use, then please give me faith to trust You with the outcome.'

"When Steve came home the next day from work, he announced that he intended to do the very thing he had insisted the night before was completely unnecessary. He had heard something on the radio which steered his heart in a different direction. The third person in my marriage, God, had been at work."

We now have forty-five years of life together, and they have reinforced the truth that one relationship (with God) determines the health of all our relationships. Praying together in a back-and-forth conversation style is central to our marriage. We have discovered that if we are transparent with God and habitually confess and repent before Him, it always spills over into our relationship with each other.

MARRIAGE POINTS TO CHRIST

I am fascinated by what the apostle Paul said about marriage between a man and a woman. In Ephesians 5:31, he quotes Genesis 2:24 related to God's definition of marriage. He then says, "This mystery is great; but I am speaking with reference to Christ and the church." Paul is thus proclaiming that every marriage is a signpost that points to the ultimate marriage God longs for us to experience in Jesus Christ.

Marriage points to the Gospel of Christ! If you review God's definition of marriage from Genesis 2:23–25, the connection between marriage and the Gospel of Christ becomes clear. As we *receive* our mate as a gift from God, so we receive Jesus Christ as God's ultimate gift to us (John 1:12–13). As we *leave* father and mother and *cleave* unto our mate, so we leave our old allegiances and false saviors and cleave unto Christ as our only Savior and Lord (1 Thessalonians 1:9). As we become *one flesh* with our marriage partner, so we become one with Jesus Christ and are members of His body (1 Corinthians12:13). And as we are *naked and not ashamed* with our marriage partner, so we are open and laid bare before God in Christ (Hebrews 4:13). When we realize that our marriage is designed by God to reflect His glory and the Gospel to the world, it takes on a new sacredness which motivates us to diligently seek to enter the harbor of marital intimacy.

The attractive appeal of a healthy marriage became bluntly obvious to me at the gym where I work out. I have a ministry with the staff at the front desk that I call "The Hope Club." I ask the person at the front desk how I can pray for them as I am working out. After my workout, I come back by and give them a few Scripture verses that align with the issues they have asked me to pray for. Many of them keep lists of these verses and share them with their co-workers.

All the front desk workers have been warm and receptive and have communicated how much they enjoyed being in The Hope Club—all except one lady, whom I mentally labeled "Frowny Face" because she was always somewhat cold and distant.

One day, I went into the gym and Frowny Face looked up at me and smiled! She then said, "Mr. King, where is your wife?" I told her she was at a school event because she is a teacher. The lady then blurted out, "Your marriage is amazing! I love the way you and your wife care for each other and are so close! What is your secret?"

I was shocked because I did not think this lady knew my name or even that I was married. However, she had been watching us for months.

I responded, "Do you really want to know what makes our marriage work?" She emphatically said, "Yes!" By this time, three or four of her co-workers had gathered around. I asked her to take out a piece of paper and number it one to three.

"First," I said, "Mae Belle and I both love Jesus Christ, and we invite Him to sit on the throne of our lives every day. We have discovered that if Jesus is on the throne of each of our lives, He will not war with Himself, and He brings us close together.

"Second, Mae Belle and I are committed to serving each other. This was part of our marriage vows, and we have discovered if we both focus on serving the other, then we are both killing our bent to selfishness, and we both have our needs met."

Then I said, "If we remove this one from our marriage, we will be in trouble in one week. It is the R word—repent. To repent means that you admit you are wrong and make it right. We both are committed to repenting and making things right with each other."

I then shared with her God's definition of marriage, tied it to Ephesians 5:31–32, and told her about Jesus Christ. This lady has been open and receptive to us ever since that day, and I am praying for her salvation.

One relationship determines the health of *all* your relationships.

I began this chapter by saying every married ministry leader must face a reality about relational priorities:

If you want to qualify as a leader worth following, your relationship with God *must* shape your relationship with your mate. If this is not consistently evident to those who follow you, then you are not qualified to lead God's people. I hope this no longer sounds blunt and hard to swallow.

The reason is that marriage is sacred, reflects the oneness of the Trinity, points to the Gospel, and is a primary way God molds us into the image of Christ.

Yet your relationship with God through Jesus Christ will outlive your marriage. That is why your relationship with God must be the one relationship that shapes all your relationships.

Any joy that we experience in marriage here on earth is a mere shadow of the joy that we will experience when we are joined together with our Lord and Savior. One day, there will be a wedding feast so joyful, so far beyond anything we could imagine—a celebration of Christ's marriage to us as His bride, His church. Scripture proclaims: "Blessed are those who are invited to the marriage supper of the Lamb" (Rev 19:9).

God designed your marriage to point to that coming union. While you have it, leverage it for the glory of God. Make up your mind, form a conviction, and let it mark you. If you want to qualify as a leader worth following, *begin* with your marriage. Start today.

WORKOUTS TO THRIVE AND FINISH STRONG

1. Review the chapter and identify what was most helpful to you. Why? Share your answers with your spouse.
2. Share with your spouse specific encouragement in terms of where they are positively living out God's

definition of marriage. What are they doing in the marriage that you especially appreciate?

3. Memorize Genesis 2:24–25 and make a "marriage box" with your spouse (see appendix for directions). Display it in your home and share its meaning with someone else. If you have children, teach them God's definition of marriage.

4. Review the chapter and identify where your marriage boat may be leaking. Why did you select these areas? Are they the same ones your spouse would pick?

5. Review your wedding vows or the ones provided here. Plan a time to officially renew your vows.

"Will you, _____, have _____ to be your husband/wife? Will you love him/her, comfort and keep him/her, and forsaking all other remain true to him/her as long as you both shall live?" ("I will")

"I _____, take you _____, to be my wedded husband/wife. To have and to hold, from this day forward, for better, for worse, for richer, for poorer, in sickness or in health, to love and to cherish till death do us part. This is my sacred vow."

6. Pray with your spouse today. Begin to make this a daily habit and "interview" your loved one to discover what way of praying they are most comfortable with. Discuss ways you can bring the unseen third partner in your marriage (God) more into the center of your relationship.

Do you have any unresolved conflicts in your marriage? Review the section on confession, memorize the suggested verses and be first to confess your sins. Do all you can to keep the unity of the Spirit in your marriage.

CHAPTER 6

Determine Your Leadership Path

He always lives to make intercession for them.

—Hebrews 7:25

The accuser of our brethren . . . accuses them before our God day and night.

—Revelation 12:10

We . . . are workers with you for your joy.

—2 Corinthians 1:24

There is a startling truth every ministry leader needs to awaken to and remember on a regular basis.

The Bible teaches and experience confirms that leaders who are ignorant of this paradigm-shifting truth or are aware of its reality yet downplay it *will eventually be sidelined.*

135

Yet those who embrace it and align their leadership with it *will thrive and finish strong.*

I was awakened to this shocking reality by a seasoned pastor just weeks before I assumed my first senior pastor role. I had served two years on the staff of the squabbling church, and after much prayer and evaluation, I had accepted the call to be their pastor.

Somewhat overwhelmed by the task before me, I met with the wise and respected mentor for insights. I found myself pouring out complaints about the "dysfunctional" church I had been called to lead.

He attentively listened and then handed me his Bible and asked me to read out loud to him the following two passages:

"Therefore, He is able also to save forever those who draw near to God through Him, since He always lives to make intercession for them" (Hebrews 7:25).

"Then I heard a loud voice in heaven, saying, 'Now the salvation, and the power, and the kingdom of our God and the authority of His Christ have come, for the accuser of our brethren has been thrown down, he who accuses them before our God day and night'" (Revelation 12:10).

He then looked me in the eye and said, "When you think of God's people in your local church, who do you align with the most—Jesus the intercessor or Satan the accuser?"

His question stunned me and awakened me to the ugly reality of who my hard heart was beginning to align with! I decided at that moment, by God's grace, always to align my leadership with Jesus the Intercessor, not Satan the accuser.

Little did I know how much I would need to embrace my new resolve to be an intercessor for God's people. A few weeks later, on a Sunday night, the church overwhelmingly voted to call me as their senior pastor. I spoke for twenty minutes, casting a vision for the future with a strong emphasis on loving God and people above all else.

After the service, a line of well-wishers welcomed me and expressed their hopes for a bright future together. A disturbed young man waited his turn. When the crowd drifted away, he walked up to me and blurted out, "You are full of bull!" with emphasis on the last word.

My response to his disdain would shape my leadership of the church family I was assigned to shepherd for the next seven years.

I told Mae Belle that I would meet her at home later and then turned and punched the young man. Just kidding! I actually invited him to join me in my study at the church.

As we sat down, I told him that I thought we were friends and that I was hurt and disappointed at his inappropriate comments to me. I knew his "hurt trail." His dad had abandoned the family when he was a boy, and the former pastor had been like a father to him. During the previous year, I had visited this young man on his college campus and spent time trying to encourage him in his faith. He had a keen mind and a heart for God but his "father wound" hung like a cloud over him and fed his tendency toward criticism. I knew he was hurting, and I had learned that hurt people hurt people. I silently prayed and decided to focus more on listening than lecturing.

I asked him what was going on in his heart that would cause him to speak to me as he did. He began to cry and explained that he was grieving over the former pastor's resignation, which had occurred a year before. This young man resented me taking the place of a man who had been like a father to him.

I walked over, sat down beside him, and gave him a hug. I told him that I also loved the former pastor and missed his presence at our church. As a matter of fact, he was a mentor to me and had been my New Testament Greek professor in my final year of seminary. I told this grieving brother that I knew I could not take the former pastor's place in his life. However, I would be his friend and seek to be a good pastor to him.

He asked me to forgive him for his outburst, and we committed to meet with each other regularly. After that night, we became friends, and I delighted in watching him grow into a faithful follower of Christ. He never treated me with disrespect again.

Who are you aligning your leadership with?

Consider how seriously God takes a leader's call to be an intercessor and not an accuser of His people. Moses led the people of God in the wilderness for forty years, and the people rebelled against God and Moses ten times. *Each time*, Moses responded by interceding for them—*except once*. For that one time, God refused to let Moses take them into the Promised Land. God refused to allow an accuser to lead His people home.

Have you considered that your leadership is *always* moving toward alignment with a very powerful person? Your assignment is to make sure that powerful person is Jesus Christ.

ANTICIPATE THE GROWTH ACCELERATORS!

I have had many "alignment assignment" opportunities since then and have given God's "extra-grace-required people" a title. I call them GAs, which stands for *growth accelerators*. This title reminds me of God's purposes in bringing "harder to love" people into my life: He is accelerating my growth and reminding me to be an intercessor and not an accuser!

It also reminds me that God is on a quest and refuses to be deterred from His holy mission. His sanctified mission includes an "alignment assignment." Romans 8:28–29 reveals both God's quest when it comes to shaping His people and our alignment assignment.

And we know that God causes all things to work together for good to those who love God, to those who are called according to His purpose. For those whom He foreknew, He also predestined to become conformed to the image of His Son, so that He would be the firstborn among many brethren.

Verse 28 is both positive and popular, but its truths cannot be properly understood without intentionally linking them to verse 29. The "good" for which God is working all things together is not just pleasant circumstances and answers to prayer. God loves to give good things to His children (James 1:17), but the good He ultimately aims at is long-lasting and deep goodness. Note that the promise in verse 28 that He is actively working "for the good of those who love God and are called according to His purpose" is firmly connected to the next verse by the word *for*—meaning *because.* God is working all things together for good on behalf of his people *because* he foreknew them and predestined them to become conformed to the image of His Son. God's quest and the goodness He is determined to pour into our lives are one and the same: to make us like Jesus Christ. He predestined us to become like Jesus and will complete His quest when we see Him face to face (1 John 3:2). However, He currently is working everything together in our lives to move us toward Christlikeness.

REPLACEMENT THINKING

Because the negative message from my first Sunday night GA was so blunt, it has permanently imprinted on my mind. I have learned to leverage his negative message for good not only by remembering God's call on me to be an intercessor but by aligning myself with God's quest to make me like Jesus.

I employ what I call "replacement thinking": I discovered that whenever my "bull brother" came to mind, I would end up mentally replaying his ugly message. So I decided to leverage this by aligning myself with Jesus. I would "replace" his negative message with truth about my identity and purpose in Christ. If I did not replace his message in my mind with a better one from God, it would dominate my thoughts and pollute my spirit.

For example, suppose I told you, "Do not think about the number three." In this scenario, three stands for the negative message you are seeking to disregard. You could promise not to do so, pray and make yourself accountable, but alas, you would not only remember the number three—it would begin to dominate your thoughts. The harder you focused on forgetting about the number three, the stronger its presence would be in your mind.

So instead, try this: Every time the number three comes to your mind, imagine it has a finger pointing to the number 5,286 divided by six. You would become so busy figuring out the new number that you would soon forget about the number three. You have defeated the domination of the number three by replacing it!

REPLACEMENT RELATIONSHIPS

A few days after my Sunday evening "bull" encounter, I had emotionally recovered. I was eager to fully engage in feeding God's people on his Word and the work of making disciples as

I embarked on my first full week on the job. Little did I know that a "GA on steroids" was about to invade my life.

I was in my study, working hard on my sermon for the coming Sunday and planning some outreach events for the coming month. My secretary and church family already knew my schedule: I devoted the hours from seven to noon to study and prayer and was available for ministry from noon on.

Suddenly, an older lady in the congregation burst into my office. She had somehow bypassed my secretary and appeared in front of my desk with her hands on her hips and a stern look on her face—a little old lady in tennis shoes! She immediately began to share her views on my previous Sunday morning sermon (which she gave good scores) and then began to berate me for the way I made announcements. She said, "The way you made announcements was stupid. Did you hear me? I said *stupid*!" Before I could respond, she turned and walked out of my office.

I was shocked, hurt, and furious. I knew if I immediately went after her that I would say and do things I should not! I could picture myself choking her, and thought it would be wonderful if hers was my first funeral! I simply could not think of anything but her awful and rude treatment of me and pondered how I should respond.

It was almost lunchtime, so I drove home and sought wisdom from Mae Belle. She patiently listened as I poured out my verbal wrath on the little old lady and shared some options for dealing with her that were clearly fueled by the accuser of the brethren!

After I wore myself out, Mae Belle said, "Guess what I was reading for devotions in my Bible this morning?" I was not in a mood to hear, but because it was coming from my best friend, who had just patiently listened to my tirade, I said, "What?" She then read aloud to me 1 Peter 3:8–9:

To sum up, all of you be harmonious, sympathetic, brotherly, kind-hearted, and humble in spirit; **not returning evil for evil or insult for insult but giving a blessing instead;** *for you were called for the very purpose that you might inherit a blessing.* (Emphasis mine.)

"That was nice," I said.

Mae Belle then leveraged the truth of 1 Peter 3:8–9, and I learned how *replacement relationships* are essential for responding to mega-GAs! She suggested that we invite the lady and her husband over for dinner that week! This would be a direct way to apply the 1 Peter passage and *replace* the insult I had received with a blessing.

At first, I protested—I had passed the test with the rude young man, and my replacement *thinking* was helping me love him. But this "mega-GA lady" was a new category. It would require a *replacement relationship*—replacing her curse with a blessing.

Mae Belle continued to appeal to me, backing it up with a reminder of our calling in Christ, and I was convicted and began to think, *This is my first week on the job. What do I have to lose?* So Mae Belle called the woman. She and her husband eagerly accepted our invitation to come to our home that week for dinner.

That evening, I got "the rest of the story." I discovered that this woman and her husband loved me and prayed for me often and longed to see me succeed as a pastor. I also learned that she had been deeply wounded by previous pastors. Her charade in my office was her way of "testing me" to see what kind of pastor I would be. This woman did love me over the seven years I spent as her pastor, and God used her to give me a heart for global missions. Because her son was a global mission leader, she led the charge in our church family to pray for missionaries and take the Gospel to those who have never heard. She is now in Heaven, but her passion to reach all peoples with the Gospel and to make sure the local church is missions-minded has been passed on to me.

I have often thought I could have wiped myself out my first week as a pastor. I could have become a bitter accuser of the brethren if it were not for the grace of God working on me through His Word and Mae Belle.

I may have given the impression that I view spiritual leadership as somewhat reactive, neglecting the counterbalance of proactive discipleship, confrontation, exhortation, and the exercise of restorative church discipline. I have learned that when we align our leadership path and purposes with the master of all leaders, Jesus Christ, we will grow in our confidence in speaking the truth in love, confronting sin, and exercising restorative discipline.

LEAD LIKE JESUS, NOT HEROD

Mark 6:1–32 contrasts the path and purposes of Jesus's leadership with that of Herod Antipas—the man who had John the Baptist beheaded. The stark contrasts in the path and purposes of Jesus and Herod should fill us with hope and fear at the same time. We only have two options before us every day as leaders: to lead the way of Jesus or to lead the way of Herod. *Our hope* grows when we remember that our union with Jesus Christ and the Holy Spirit compels us to lead the God-glorifying way of Jesus. *Our fear* is fueled when we realize the culture we swim in, combined with our own sin-bents, entices us to lead in the self-glorifying way of Herod.

Before we explore these two radically different leadership paths, I have a confession to make. Even though I have studied leadership extensively and have led as a senior pastor for more than forty years, it was only ten years ago that I stopped borrowing definitions of spiritual leadership and developed my own. A decade ago, I teamed with eight other leaders to scripturally define spiritual leadership. We then designed a process for multiplying healthy ministry leaders.

As we studied the Scriptures, our thinking evolved from seeing leadership as simply influence to seeing it as *Christ-shaped* influence. Eventually, we realized the difference between influence and leadership: Though every believer is a person of influence, not every believer is a leader. The difference between influence and leadership is revealed in our definition of a spiritual leader.

Spiritual leaders are shaped by Christ to equip and mobilize others to fulfill God's purposes.

Read that definition again and consider its implications for your leadership. Following this definition demands that one abandon the way of Herod and intentionally follow both the path and the purposes of Jesus. *The path* is intentionally being shaped by Jesus Christ. *The purposes* are to equip and mobilize others to fulfill God's purposes.

The order is essential because if you are not intentionally being shaped by Christ, then you are being shaped more by your culture, background, personality, and preferences than by Jesus. And if you are not intentionally being shaped by Christ to fulfill His purposes, then you may mobilize and equip people, but not in a way that necessarily aligns with His purposes. This approach demands a consistent commitment to His lordship, which includes being shaped by the Word of God, the Spirit of God, and the people of God.

It is so helpful to learn from leaders who have embraced the path of *Christ-shaped leadership*. Johnathan Edwards (1703–1758) was such a leader. He is widely regarded as America's most important theologian and a seasoned pastor who played a critical role in shaping the First Great Awakening. However, while the flames of revival were spreading from England all across the U.S., Edwards was having major troubles in his church. His salary had been withheld for over two years, he was eventually fired over a doctrinal dispute, and his daughter died. The man who led the charge to run Edwards out said of him, "Mister Edward's joy during this season was out of reach because it rested in eternity." Edwards grounded his hope in the Gospel and joyfully persevered through the pain. He thrived and finished strong.[1]

THE PATH AND PURPOSES OF JESUS-LIKE LEADERSHIP

Let's explore the path and purposes of Jesus-like leadership as revealed in Mark 6.

Jesus's disciples did not follow him because of his position and status in society; he was an itinerate rabbi and carpenter. They were compelled to follow Him based solely on His moral authority.

Jesus went out from there and came into His hometown; and His disciples followed Him (Mark 6:1).

Jesus developed his moral authority over a period of thirty years in a disciplined walk with God.

And Jesus kept increasing in wisdom and stature, and in favor with God and men (Luke 2:52).

For example, in Nazareth, Jesus relied on moral authority to respond to misinformed and stinging criticism. His clear conscience and confidence in His identity shielded Him from an ungodly response.

When the Sabbath came, He began to teach in the synagogue; and the many listeners were astonished, saying, "Where did this man get these things, and what is this wisdom given to Him, and such miracles as these performed by His hands? Is not this the carpenter, the son of Mary, and brother of James and Joses and Judas and Simon? Are not His sisters here with us?" And they took offense at Him. Jesus said to them, "A prophet is not without honor except in his hometown and among his own relatives and in his own household (Mark 6:2–4).

As a builder of disciples, Jesus trained by modeling and empowering. Although clearly a missions-minded and visionary leader, Jesus never made His disciples feel like pawns for His plans. Instead, following Jesus resulted in being empowered and equipped to fulfill God's purposes. First, He modeled a holistic approach to ministry with preaching, healing, and serving, and then He sent them in teams to go and do what they had seen him do.

And He summoned the twelve and began to send them out in pairs, and gave them authority over the unclean spirits; and He instructed them that they should take nothing for their journey, except a mere staff—no bread, no bag, no money in their belt—but to wear sandals; and He added, "Do not put on two tunics." And He said to them, "Wherever you enter a house, stay there until you leave town. Any place that does not receive you or listen to you, as you go out from there, shake the dust off the soles of your feet for a testimony against them." They went out and preached that men should repent. And they were casting out many demons and were anointing with oil many sick people and healing them (Mark 6:7–13).

Following Jesus both fed their faith in God and fostered effective teamwork. Jesus's disciples were not only empowered by Him, but they were also accountable to Him. At the end of their mission, they reported back to Him.

They went out and preached that men should repent. And they were casting out many demons and were anointing with oil many sick people and healing them. The apostles gathered together with Jesus; and they reported to Him all that they had done and taught (Mark 6:12–13, 30).

Then, ever the servant leader, Jesus cared for his band of brothers and urged them to rest, modeling a balanced life and preserving an emotionally healthy team.

And He said to them, "Come away by yourselves to a secluded place and rest a while." (For there were many people coming and going, and they did not even have time to eat.) They went away in the boat to a secluded place by themselves (Mark 6:31–32).

Jesus was shaped by His heavenly Father to equip and mobilize His disciples to fulfill the Father's purposes. The perfect model for all leaders, He led by relying on His moral authority, training through modeling, empowering followers, expecting accountability, and nurturing the personal lives of those on his team.

THE PATH AND PURPOSES OF HEROD-LIKE LEADERSHIP

Herod Antipas's leadership stands in stark contrast with Jesus's. Even though Herod had status and authority as a king, he lacked moral authority. He was ruled by his violated conscience. While shoring up his power in Rome, he had an affair with Herodias, his half-brother Philip's wife. Herod then divorced his first wife, married his brother's wife, and became a stepfa-ther.[2] His violated conscience would pollute his leadership and put him in a position to be manipulated.

And King Herod heard of it, for His name had become well known; and people were saying, "John the Baptist has risen from the dead, and that is why these miraculous powers are at work in Him." But others were saying, "He is Elijah." And others were saying, "He is a prophet, like one of the prophets of old." But when Herod heard of it, he kept saying, "John, whom I beheaded, has risen!" (Mark 6:14–16).

Herod had an encounter with John the Baptist, a leader whose moral authority both attracted and convicted him. John the Baptist courageously confronted Herod about his unlawful marriage to Herodias. Herod's response to this "justice-based criticism" revealed his abuse of power and manipulative leader-ship style. Herod, spurred on by his wife, Herodias, imprisoned John. However, even though John was physically confined, it was Herod who was held captive by the iron bars of his own violated conscience.

For Herod himself had sent and had John arrested and bound in prison because of Herodias, the wife of his brother Philip, because he had married her. For John had been saying to Herod, "It is not lawful for you to have your brother's wife." Herodias had a grudge against him and wanted to put him to death and could not do so (Mark 6:17–19).

In contrast, John's clear conscience and moral authority gave him a platform to urge Herod to break free from his me-first leadership style.

[F]or Herod was afraid of John, knowing that he was a righteous and holy man, and he kept him safe. And when he heard him, he was very perplexed; but he used to enjoy listening to him (Mark 6:20).

But Herodias knew how to manipulate Herod's selfish, sensual, and self-destructive leadership, using her own daughter as a pawn to push Herod to "save face" by removing John's head!

A strategic day came when Herod on his birthday gave a banquet for his lords and military commanders and the leading men of Galilee; and when the daughter of Herodias herself came in and danced, she pleased Herod and his dinner guests; and the king said to the girl, "Ask me for whatever you want and I will give it to you." And he swore to her, "Whatever you ask of me, I will give it to you; up to half of my kingdom." And she went out and said to her mother, "What shall I ask for?" And she said, "The head of John the Baptist." Immediately she came in a hurry to the king and asked, saying, "I want you to give me at once the head of John the Baptist on a platter." And although the king was very sorry, yet because of his oaths and because of his dinner guests, he was unwilling to refuse her. Immediately the king sent an executioner and commanded him to bring back his head. And he went and had him beheaded in the prison, and brought his head on a platter, and gave it to the girl; and the girl gave it to her mother. When his disciples heard about this, they came and took away his body and laid it in a tomb (Mark 6:21–29).

Herod would remain imprisoned by his violated conscience and would eventually lose his position and die in exile.[3] His leadership style showcases the folly of violating our conscience and mobilizing others to serve our own selfish purposes. While Jesus nurtured his team, Herod destructively manipulated his.

Warren Wiersbe, in his insightful book *Meet Your Conscience*, captures the essence of what the New Testament tells us about how our conscience functions. It operates as both a window and a judge. As a window, our conscience lets the light of God in, but the conscience itself is not the light.[4]

The eye is the lamp of the body; so then, if your eye is clear, your whole body will be full of light. But if your eye is bad, your whole body will be full of darkness. If then the light that is in you is darkness, how great is the darkness! (Matthew 6:22–23).

As a judge, our conscience bears witness to the law in our heart, but is not itself the law.

For when Gentiles who do not have the Law do instinctively the things of the Law, these, not having the Law, are a law to themselves, in that they show the work of the Law written in their hearts, their conscience bearing witness and their thoughts alternately accusing or else defending them, on the day when, according to my gospel, God will judge the secrets of men through Christ Jesus (Romans 2:14–16).

Each time we violate our conscience, the window that lets in the light is smudged, and the judge sees less and less. Therefore, we can progressively develop a weak, defiled, evil, and seared conscience.

*However not all men have this knowledge; but some, being accustomed to the idol until now, eat food as if it were sacrificed to an idol; and their conscience being **weak is defiled*** (1 Corinthians 8:7, emphasis mine).

*Let us draw near with a sincere heart in full assurance of faith, having our hearts sprinkled clean from an **evil** conscience and our bodies washed with pure water* (Hebrews 10:22, emphasis mine).

*[B]y means of the hypocrisy of liars **seared** in their own conscience as with a branding iron* (1 Timothy 4:2, emphasis mine).

On the other hand, we can strengthen our conscience by knowing our identity in Christ and aligning our lives with our union with Christ in the power of the Holy Spirit. This leads to developing a progressively healthy conscience—strong, clean, good, and blameless.

*But the goal of our instruction is love from a pure heart and a **good** conscience and a sincere faith* (1 Timothy 1:5, emphasis mine).

*[K]eeping faith and a **good** conscience, which some have rejected and suffered shipwreck in regard to their faith* (1 Timothy 1:19, emphasis mine).

*[B]ut holding to the mystery of the faith with a **clear** conscience* (1 Timothy 3:9, emphasis mine).

*[L]et us draw near with a sincere heart in full assurance of faith, having our hearts sprinkled **clean** from an evil conscience and our bodies washed with pure water* (Hebrews 10::22, emphasis mine).

*In view of this, I also do my best to maintain always a **blameless** conscience both before God and before men* (Acts 24:16, emphasis mine).

As leaders, we have only two options before us each day: lead the way of Jesus or the way of Herod.

Be hopeful: Our union with Jesus Christ and the Holy Spirit compels us to lead the way of Jesus.

Be fearful: Our culture and sin-bent hearts entice us to lead the way of Herod.

Determine to be a leader who is shaped by Christ to equip and mobilize others to fulfill God's purposes. Daily turn your back on leadership that is shaped by the selfishness that uses others to fulfill your own purposes.

WORKOUTS TO THRIVE AND FINISH STRONG

1. Review the chapter and teach the core principles to someone else.

   Jesus, the perfect model for all leaders, led by relying on His moral authority, training through modeling, empowering followers, expecting accountability, and nurturing the personal lives of those on his team. Jesus lived for the glory of God.

Herod's leadership style showcases the folly of violating our conscience, manipulating others, and mobilizing them to serve our own selfish purposes. Herod lived for his own glory.

Our Two Leadership Options
Mark 6:1–32

The Way of Jesus	The Way of Herod
Moral authority	Authority in position
Foundation = trust in God	Foundation = self-protection
Empowerment of others	Uses others for selfish purposes
Gives away authority	Clings to authority
Clear conscience forged by accountability to God and others	Defiled conscience, refusing accountability to God and others.
Servant who nurtures the team	Manipulator who uses the team

2. I have read several dozen books on leadership that practice the principle of "eating the meat and discarding the bones" (Hebrews 5:14). One of my favorite books that has far more meat than bone is *Spiritual Leadership* by Henry and Richard Blackaby (Broadman & Holman Publishers, 2001). Chapter 4 is worth the book—"The Leader's Vision: Where Do Leaders Get It and How Do They Communicate It?" The Blackabys outline six sources of vision that are not rooted in God's

character, purposes, or Word. They then focus on God's revelation, in His Word, as a source of vision.

This has been a paradigm shift for me and has been both liberating and challenging. It is essential that spiritual leaders walk closely with God, know His purposes from His Word, and model learning how to join God in His work. I suggest you obtain the Blackabys' book and read it with a discerning mind.

When I first came to Cherrydale, the church was in debt, divided, and had been on a downward trend for seven years. I carried a 3x5 card in my pocket, and as I went through the week, I used it to record places where I saw God at work. On Sundays, I wove these "God at work among us" stories into my messages. This changed the church family's focus from themselves and the decline they were experiencing to God and His work among us. Soon they began to capture the joy of joining Jesus in His work, and a movement was launched which continues to this day.

3. Over the years, I have come to value the benefits of working with a team and have embraced the biblical model of a team of elders with a lead pastor overseeing and shepherding God's flock. The core principles are outlined in the paper found in the appendix under "A Team of Elders with a Lead Pastor."

CHAPTER 7

Walk with a
Band of Brothers

"Without friends, no one would want to live, even if he had all other goods."

—Aristotle

"Never hold resentments for the person who tells you what you need to hear; count them among your truest, most caring, and valuable friends."

—Mike Norton, *Just Another War Story*

As leaders, it's imperative that we don't try to go it alone. Seek out a band of brothers. Serve them, love them, fight for them, and allow them to do the same for you.

The truth is that it is impossible for a leader to stay on track without friends. Heed the African proverb: If you want to go fast, go alone. If you want to go far, go together.

Face it, *not* seeking out authentic friendships is going against the way God designed you. You were made in the image of an eternal band of brothers—Father, Son, and Holy Spirit—and therefore you were made for relationship (Genesis 1:1–28). Jesus was the Son of God, yet He intentionally walked with a band of brothers. He did not go it alone!

CULTIVATE FRIENDSHIPS AND FIND A BAND OF BROTHERS

The National Institute of Health (NIH) has conducted many studies on the power of healthy friendships, and it has consistently found they are linked with lower risks of heart attacks and other stress-related illnesses, thus leading to longer life. On the other hand, loneliness and social isolation are coupled with poorer health, depression, and an increased risk of early death.

Proverbs has one up on the NIH because its inspired instructions tell us how to attract and maintain healthy friendships. It makes leaders face reality: Your friends will make or break your life. "He who walks with wise men will be wise, but the companion of fools will suffer harm" (Proverbs 13:20). Friends walk together and build their relationship around common core values. C.S. Lewis, in his essay on friendship, says that friends ask, "What, you too?"

Proverbs gives us five traits of a healthy friend. Make up your mind to *be* a "Proverbs kind of friend," and you will *attract* this kind of friend.

A good object lesson to help you remember these traits is a box labeled "A Healthy Friend Is . . ." Place the objects detailed below in the box. Teach and model these to your kids and infuse them into the fabric of your ministry; your ability to fulfill your mission is partially built on whether you consistently apply these five traits.

COMMITTED (ELMER'S GLUE)

Mutual commitment is the mark of a healthy friendship. "A friend loves at all times, and a brother is born for adversity" (Proverbs 17:17). A friend can not only see you through your troubles, but *love* you to the other side of them.

Think about concentric circles, starting with physical brothers (if you have them) and moving outward. Your objective is not just to get your needs met but to learn to love and serve others who can walk the path of life with you for the glory of God.

Every year, my two literal brothers and I go away for a "brothers' retreat" and have so much fun we wind up laughing so hard it hurts. During those two to three days together, we share our true heart issues. What we share does not go outside our brother circle. Fortunately, we all love Jesus and can bring both our brotherhood and the Gospel into our relationship. We pray, claim promises, discuss the Scriptures, and help each other learn how to apply the Gospel to our hearts. We have walked with each other through the deaths of our grandparents, cousins, and father. The three of us have been there for each other through losing a business and starting over, alcohol addiction and recovery, a son who announced he is gay, learning to hold truth and love well, various diseases and recoveries, and a long list of highs and joys in life. We each know we have brothers who love us and will tell us hard truth.

I just returned from a walk with my good friend, John. Every other Friday morning, we walk together for over an hour. Sometimes we ride bikes or kayak on the Potomac. During that time, we sing, pray, share the issues we are working through, and encourage each other to apply the Gospel to every area of our lives. We talk through issues in the news, books we have read, problems we are trying to solve—and all the while, we are loving the outdoor exercise. We have known each other for over twenty years, and he is indeed a friend who sticks closer than a brother. Both of us come away from our walks refreshed and can hardly wait for the next one. Our "iron sharpening iron" time has helped us both spot and plug the slow leaks in our character.

CONSIDERATE (DEODORANT)

"He who blesses his friend with a loud voice early in the morning, it will be reckoned a curse to him" (Proverbs 27:14). Healthy friends read each other's needs and respond accordingly.

Four months ago, I conducted the funeral of one of my close friends, one I have called "Dad" for over twenty-five years. When his beloved Martha was on her deathbed, she and Ralph told me they wanted to "adopt" me as their son. After I conducted her funeral, Ralph said, "Son, you have a free staff member."

He took over our tape ministry (now it is online), oversaw our radio ministries, and did a thousand odd jobs around the church. He was my wise counselor and confidante. He helped me gut my home and put it back together again in five weeks, and all along the way, he mentored me in home improvement projects. He never once put demands on me and always sought out ways to serve me. The black briefcase I carry around is worn and tattered, but I will never get rid of it because Ralph gave it to me.

He was the epitome of a considerate friend. I want to be like him.

CONFIDENTIAL (A KEY)

"He who goes about as a talebearer reveals secrets, but he who is trustworthy conceals a matter" (Proverbs 11:13). "A perverse man spreads strife, and a slanderer separates intimate friends" (Proverbs 16:28).

Your secrets are under lock and key with a healthy friend. The truth is that, if someone will gossip *to* you, they will gossip *about* you.

When we were a young married couple living all the way across the country from our families, Mae Belle and I had our first son, Joshua. Mae Belle needed a friend and looked for a godly woman she could trust. That friendship lasted for over thirty years until her friend went to Heaven.

I worked side-by-side with Bob for twenty-seven years; he served as our missions pastor and executive pastor. He knows everything about me and loves me anyway. Not once in those twenty-seven years did he betray a confidence. I often say of him, "I would turn everything I have over to him and have zero concerns."

CANDID (MIRROR)

"Faithful are the wounds of a friend, but deceitful are the kisses of an enemy" (Proverbs 27:6).

A true friend cares more about your welfare than the tension that may result from telling you the truth. I've had several friends like that—and in fact, once they all came together to tell me some hard truths at the same time!

I call it my 666 day: June 6, 2006. Our pastoral team had gathered for our weekly meeting, and after prayer and dealing with key items on our agenda, they asked if they could speak with me. I was in the habit of speaking frankly with them and was honestly eager to hear what they had to say. I pulled out my notepad and tuned in. Their tone was loving and respectful, yet I sensed this might not be good news. Essentially, they said this:

"We love and respect you and will follow you through a brick wall. But there are aspects of your leadership style that need to change. You tend, at times, to be overly controlling, you have a bent toward people-pleasing, and you can be impulsive. These patterns are hurting us and making it hard to function as a healthy team."

I listened, asked a few clarifying questions, and thanked them for sharing with me. Later that day, I shared with Mae Belle what they had told me. I secretly thought she would say they had overstated the case and would rally to my side by emphasizing all my other positive traits. My sweetheart listened carefully, affirmed me, and then said, "They told you the truth."

For some reason, I kept remembering verses from Proverbs that I did not want to come into my mind at that time! They were passages about the fool who does not listen to rebuke and the wise man who welcomes it.[1]

The team I was working with and Mae Belle had "held up the mirror" to help me face what I did not want to see. I had to face some hard "grace-based" truth and either cooperate with Jesus to change—or quit. I went into my study, licked my wounds, and asked Jesus to change me.

The next day, I asked the pastors to meet with me. I told them that what they shared was painful, but they were right, and Mae Belle affirmed their assessment. I asked for their prayer and told them that by the grace of God, I would seek to change. Over the years, this has changed the culture of our team to be open and deal with "the elephants in the room." It is freeing to live in an environment where we can admit our weaknesses and lean on each other.

CONSTRUCTIVE (HAMMER)

"Iron sharpens iron, so one man sharpens another" (Proverbs 27:17).

I believe either leading or participating in a weekly small group is one of the best ways for leaders to thrive and finish strong. Every year, I prayerfully ask a team of men in our local church to meet with me in a small group from the fall till the next summer. I let them know in advance what the time commitment will be, what our mission is, and what is expected. This keeps me in touch with others who can speak into my life and helps multiply leaders. A sample of what our small group agreement looks like is included at the end of this chapter for your use.

Paul paints a beautiful picture of holy unity in Ephesians 2:21: "In [Christ Jesus] the whole building [believers in Christ], being *fitted together*, is growing into a holy temple in the Lord." Paul is writing to Ephesian Christians and is metaphorically referring to the construction process used in building some of the magnificent stone temples in Ephesus. The massive stones were rubbed together, which produced friction and heat and sanded off rough surfaces until they fit together perfectly without mortar. More than two thousand years later, some of the stone buildings they *fitted together* are still standing. What a picture of God rubbing us together in relationships, which often produces friction and rubs off our rough edges, to form a holy temple where He can be at home!

Leaders don't go it alone. Join God in His holy temple building by intentionally seeking to *be* a healthy friend, and then you will *attract* healthy friends.

How do we reconcile our longing for friends and our failure at being a healthy friend?

We all *long* for the ideal friend, and we all know that we have *failed* to be the ideal friend. What are we to do?

Wise leaders face reality: Jesus Christ is the *only* ideal friend Who will perfectly satisfy our longings. Jesus Christ *alone* forgives our failures in friendship and gives us the power and motivation to be a true friend.

John, the disciple whom Jesus loved, recorded Jesus's *command* to love each other as He has loved us (John 15:12, 17). He also declared our *motivation* to love each other —"Greater love has no one than this, that one lay down his life for his friends" (John 15:13). Jesus is the true friend Who always takes us in and never lets us down.

Be a leader who walks with a band of brothers. Make this a hallmark of the ministry you lead, and look beyond your part of God's kingdom to the body of Christ in your community.

KINGDOM PARTNERSHIPS

Are you longing for a safe place in your city to experience ongoing encouragement, equipping, and motivation for ministry with other pastors and ministry leaders? Read the following testimonies from pastors and ministry leaders who have experienced "consistent renewal" by participating in our local pastors' group in Arlington, called The Band of Brothers. Do these appeal to you?

"I was tempted to quit the ministry three times in the last ten years. Each time, my calling was renewed for one reason—the Band of Brothers." —Matt M.

"As a new church planter, nothing has helped me more than to get to know my fellow pastors in the area and know that we are fighting together for the Gospel. It is hard to imagine what ministry

in this challenging mission field would be like without this network!"—Scott S.

"The Band of Brothers has been a place of safety and encouragement in my calling. The accountability and inspiring example of kingdom-mindedness is an invaluable and irreplaceable gift. It has sustained many of us in personal and ministry-related ways."—Carlos D.

"The Band of Brothers is a regular reminder that we are all in this together and that our church is part of a much, much larger story."—John S.

"I always come away from our Band of Brothers encouraged and blessed, receiving more than I give." —Drew H.

"The Band of "Brothers" has been important to me, as a woman clergyperson, since it signals an acceptance by the other leaders in the Body of Christ that I am to be treated as an equal partner." —Beth G.

"The Band of Brothers has the common goal of seeing this region transformed by the Gospel and the common experience of being transformed as we walk together in the Gospel." —Jason C.

I have had the joy of leading our Band of Brothers for the past thirty years. The testimonies you just read are only a few among many from these co-laborers in Christ. Over time, I have discovered six essentials for forming, leading, and sustaining a Christ-honoring group of pastors and ministry leaders. I call them The Six Cs.

CONVICTION

Conviction is essential if one is to effectively persuade pastors and ministry leaders to habitually come together for prayer, encouragement, and ministry. A conviction is a core belief that does not change with pressure, as opposed to a preference, which fluctuates with circumstances. My biblically based convictions have pushed me through dozens of quitting points for over thirty years and compelled me to persevere in bringing pastors and ministry leaders together. Before you attempt to do that, shore up your convictions!

- Are you *convinced* that Jesus Christ established His church to advance His kingdom around the world (Matthew 16:18, Acts 1:8)?
- Are you *held by a conviction* that Gospel-centered local churches must work together to fulfill our biblical mandate to make disciples of all people (Matthew 28:18–20)?
- Do you *truly believe* that Gospel-centered local churches are not in competition with each other but are co-laborers together (Acts 15, Ephesians 3:20–21)?
- Are you *persuaded* that part of God's call on your life is to intentionally partner with other Gospel-centered churches to seek the welfare of the city you are in (Jeremiah 29:7, Matthew 5:16)?

CONNECTION

Connection with other pastors and ministry leaders must be rooted in genuine care for each other. Start with the ones you know or the ones in your community that you should know. Share your convictions by modeling your message; genuinely seek to get to know your co-laborers in Christ. Listen, learn, love, and pray.

When I first attempted to start a fellowship, I tried to build it around a National Association of Evangelicals doctrinal statement. Everyone in our group could sign the document without hesitation, but I discovered this was not the place to start. It created an environment in which we were trying to label and categorize each other. When I shifted the focus to relationship first, then the doctrinal agreements on the essentials of the faith were naturally revealed in the context of friends who knew and trusted each other.

Progress will occur at the speed of trust, and trust is built over time in a relational context. Share your convictions and dream together. What would it look like if the pastors and ministry leaders loved each other and worked together to advance the Gospel in your community?

CONSISTENCY

Consistency is essential for building trust and advancing the Gospel together. Over the years, I have tried to bring pastors together in various settings: monthly gatherings for lunch and prayer; biweekly meetings for fellowship and encouragement; and weekly gatherings for prayer, encouragement, and ministry planning. We have tried rotating the gathering place so that different pastors host and thus "own" the fellowship. Over time, we have developed a pattern that provides consistency: we meet weekly at the same place from seven-thirty to nine o'clock on Wednesday mornings. Pastors and ministry leaders are busy, and providing a consistent place to meet each week makes it easy to stay connected with each other.

I have learned that consistent communication with the "band of brothers" has been helpful. I send out an email message before each weekly gathering and pass along ministry ideas and resources. Brothers have learned that they can count on the rest of the band being there for them.

CHRIST-CENTEREDNESS

Christ-centeredness is a non-negotiable! There are many needs and pressing issues in our communities that could bring us together, but nothing trumps Christ-centeredness. When Jesus Christ is in the center, we are compelled to humble ourselves, love each other, value differences, and persevere in working together.

We have discovered a format for our weekly meetings which naturally reinforces Christ-centeredness. After greeting each other, we invite a brother to open in prayer, and then we each share "a word from The Word"—an insight, a promise, or a teaching that has been meaningful in the last week. I often jot down notes and am fascinated to get a front-row seat each week to what God is revealing to the shepherds of His flock in our area. After we share "a word from The Word," we ask one of the pastors to lead us in prayer for the advancement of the Gospel in our area.

Next, we divide into groups of two or three to share our hearts and pray for each other. We often share "highs and lows" from the week, and the others sincerely listen. Once a brother shares, another one prays for him. This format enables each person to be heard and prayed for, and at the same time, it reinforces the Christ-centered call to listen and pray for others.

Jesus said He came to seek and to save the lost (Luke 19:10) and told his disciples, "Follow Me and I will make you fishers of men" (Mark 1:17). Being Christ-centered compels us to work together to take the Gospel in word and deed to every person in our metro area.

CO-LABOR

Co-laboring is both a mindset and a learned skill. It is so easy to focus only on our own local churches and ministries and not invest any time in "kingdom" work. Consider "tithing" your time each week to connect with other pastors and ministry leaders for advancing the Gospel in your area. At my own church, we include in our pastoral prayer each week one of our "co-laboring" Band of Brothers local churches. In addition, I mention in messages what God is doing in our area through the Band of Brothers. These simple steps have always encouraged our flock and reminded them that we are not in this alone.

We have experienced great joy and fruit in learning to co-labor together.

- An organization called *Bridge Builders* was born from the connections pastors made with each other in the Band of Brothers. Bridge Builders focuses on South Arlington and ministers to international pastors, day-laborers, and low-income residents.
- Our "Kids Camp" serves 170 children each week for eight weeks. Because of the connections formed in the Band of Brothers, we were able to partner with two other pastors who launched their own children's camps.
- On Good Friday, our churches gather for a joint worship service. What a joy to come together as the body of Christ in Arlington County! We take a collection each year at the service for a Christ-honoring ministry in our area.
- Once a year, the pastors go away together for a Prayer Summit.
- When church members drift from one of our churches to another (I call this "shifting sheep" ministry!), we are committed to making sure that relationships in the previous church are solid, and we confirm that their pastor has blessed the transfer.

- When people needing financial assistance go from church to church looking for help, we can connect with each other and ensure that support is given in a helpful way.
- Pastors who move away often launch their own "Band of Brothers" in their new locations.

CHRIST IS HONORED!

Our goal is to honor Jesus Christ by obeying the Great Command to love God and people above all else (Matthew 22:37–40) and the Great Commission to make disciples of all peoples (Matthew 28:18–20).

We are learning how to honor Jesus Christ together in the power of the Holy Spirit for the welfare of our city (Jeremiah 29:7). We believe doing so puts the glorious Gospel of Jesus Christ on display and fulfills our calling (John 13:34–35, Matthew 5:16). We are seeking to discover where Jesus is already working in our area and join Him in His work (John 5:17). This involves intentionally walking with Him each day, faithfully shepherding His flock, paying attention to the needs in our community, and staying connected with other pastors and ministry leaders.

Jesus is building His church and chasing Hell back to its gates (Matthew 16:18)! Let's press on together!

WORKOUTS TO THRIVE AND FINISH STRONG

1. Use a concordance or do a Bible word search on the words "fool" and "foolishness" from Proverbs. Discover the source of foolishness, the traits of a fool, and how to avoid this path.

2. Read the article "The Cross and Criticism" by Alfred Poirier (https://faculty.wts.edu/wp-content/uploads/2018/04/The-Cross-and-Criticism-Alfred-J.-Poirier.pdf) and identify three specific ways you can apply its insights to your life this week. Share what you learned and how you plan to apply it with someone you trust.

3. Use a concordance or do a Bible word search on the wise person from Proverbs. What are the traits of a wise person, and how is the wisdom obtained?

4. Become a part of a weekly small group in your local church or start one of your own. A sample of my weekly men's small group study is outlined below for your use. I have discovered that it is important to have a clearly stated and agreed-on mission, basic commitments, and start and stop time for the group (I have discovered nine-month groups to be effective). Mine is a men's multiply group, but the basic principles apply in various settings.

Multiply Small Group

September—June

Mission: To grow together in becoming multiplying disciples of Jesus Christ (2 Timothy 2:2) who obey the great command (Matthew 22:37–40) and the great commission (Matthew 28:18–20) in the power of the Holy Spirit, for the glory of God.

Resources: The Bible, *Multiply* by Francis Chan, and other resources to be provided

Basic Commitments:

1. Commit to grow with the group in fulfilling our mission, attend the meetings, and always have your homework done.
2. Spend time daily in God's Word and prayer. We will memorize a passage or passages of Scripture each week.
3. Faithfully pray for others and seek opportunities to share your faith and disciple others.
4. Be faithful, available, teachable, and confidential.
5. Commit to multiply. Share what you learn with others with the aim of becoming a disciple of Jesus who makes disciples of Jesus.
6. Make a commitment to our local church. If you are not a member, become one.

Meetings:

We will meet weekly, September to June, on Monday mornings from 6:00 to 7:30 a.m.

We will also meet in my home once a month in the evening (shift our Monday a.m. those weeks to the p.m. meeting). This will give us the opportunity to share a meal and have our wives join us.

We will seek to connect with each other outside group time for fellowship and ministry.

We will skip meetings during the weeks of Thanksgiving, Christmas, and Memorial Day.

CHAPTER 8

Don't Lose Heart!

*Behind **every** "lose heart" circumstance is God's "strong heart" provision.*

E ngage in ministry leadership, and you will meet the "five horsemen of the dark"—doubts, disappointments, failures, fears, and comparing yourself to others (the DDFFC).

Have you been wrestling with *Doubts* and *Disappointments?*

Do you have *Failures* from your past polluting your thoughts in the present?

Do you have *Fears* regarding your future?

Do you tend to *Compare* yourself with others and lose perspective?

If you did not say yes to all these questions, you need prayer support to get over your denial!

All ministry leaders who thrive and finish strong must learn how to wage war with the DDFFC.

Good news! Jesus Christ is on duty and eager to equip every leader who signs up to follow Him. His restorative ministry to two leaders among His own disciples who were run over by the DDFFC is extremely helpful to us.

Jesus's renewal of *doubting* and *disappointed* Thomas and the *failed*, *fearful*, and *comparison-prone* Peter took place *after* His resurrection. This indicates a pattern of how the risen Christ works in *our* lives when *we* need restoration.

JESUS RESTORES DOUBTING AND DISAPPOINTED THOMAS

But Thomas, one of the twelve, called Didymus, was not with them when Jesus came. So the other disciples were saying to him, "We have seen the Lord!" But he said to them, "Unless I see in His hands the imprint of the nails and put my finger into the place of the nails, and put my hand into His side, I will not believe." After eight days His disciples were again inside, and Thomas with them. Jesus came, the doors having been shut, and stood in their midst and said, "Peace be with you." *Then He said to Thomas,* "Reach here with your finger, and see My hands; and reach here your hand and put it into My side; and do not be unbelieving, but believing." *Thomas answered and said to Him,* "My Lord and my God!" *Jesus said to him,* "Because you have seen Me, have you believed? Blessed are they who did not see, and yet believed." (John 20:24–29)

Doubt lives in a neighborhood with words like unbelief, skepticism, suspicion, and disappointment. We don't expect these terms to be embedded in the New Testament accounts of Jesus's resurrection. So you may find it surprising, as I did, to discover them there: Matthew tells us that the eleven disciples who saw the risen Christ in Galilee worshiped him, but some were *doubtful* (Matthew 28:16–17). Mark's account reports that when Mary Magdalene told the disciples she had seen Jesus alive, they *refused to believe* her, and they *would not believe* the two who reported seeing Jesus while walking in the country (Mark 16:9–13). Luke declares that when the women reported to the disciples that Jesus had appeared to them, they *considered their words nonsense and they would not believe them* (Luke 24:11). Luke then reports that when Jesus appeared to them, spoke and showed them His hands and feet, they *still could not believe it* because of their joy and amazement (Luke 24:40–41). John records doubting Thomas's emphatic line in the sand: "Unless I see in His hands the imprint of the nails and put my finger into the place of the nails, and put my hand into His side, *I will not believe*" (John 20:25). These records of the doubts and unbelief Jesus's followers had about His resurrection are marks of the account's authenticity and a source of encouragement to us.

THREE HABITS TO CONFRONT DOUBT AND UNBELIEF

Jesus's restoration of Thomas's faith reveals three grace-based habits we need to ingrain into our lives to deal with doubt and unbelief when they come knocking.

Thomas was not present when Jesus appeared to the other disciples. (See what happens when you miss church!) A back-and-forth exchange between the disciples who had seen Jesus and Thomas ended with Thomas declaring that he would not believe unless he saw and touched the risen Christ. Thomas did not suddenly become a "show me" doubter. There were expectations he fed which, when not met, led him to the "I will not believe until" stance.

As a ministry leader, you need to pay close attention to your expectations. Expectations can often destroy relationships because when they are not met, the door flies open for disappointment and doubt to move in and make themselves at home. It happened to Thomas, and it can happen to us.

EXAMINE THE CAUSE

A study of what proceeded Thomas's "line in the sand" reveals the first habit we need in order to confront doubt: examine the cause (John 20:24–25).

John 11 tells us that when Jesus was informed of the death of his friend, Lazarus, He announced that He was going back into the area where those who sought to kill Him resided. Thomas speaks up and says, "Let us also go that we may die with him" (John 11:16). The one thing Thomas would not tolerate was being apart from Jesus, even if it meant dying with Him.

John 14 reports that Jesus told His disciples that He was going to leave them, prepare a place for them, and then come back for them. Thomas then pleaded, "Lord, we do not know where You are going; how do we know the way?" Thomas ignored the promise Jesus gave them and focused on losing the presence of Jesus (John 14:1–5).

Declaring "Unless I see *in His hands the imprint of the nails* and put my finger *into the place of the nails*, and put my hand *into His side*, I will not believe" reveals that Thomas watched Jesus die—and with Jesus's death, his faith died, too. What he feared the most—losing the presence of Jesus—came true! Thomas had stepped out onto the ice of faith, and it broke underneath him. He would not risk disappointment again unless he could touch the risen body of Jesus and know He was alive.

Do you identify with Thomas? He had trusted and been disappointed. Therefore, he was fearful of trusting again and was committed to "playing it safe."

TWO KINDS OF DOUBTERS

The good news is that the Bible reveals two kinds of doubters. The issue is not *if* we have doubt, but what *kind* we have. One God condemns, and the other He consoles.

The doubt God condemns is *dishonest* doubt because it is actually rebellion hiding behind the label of doubt. Those with rebellious unbelief cannot find God for the same reason a thief cannot find a policeman (John 3:19). Defiant unbelievers do not want God to exist and thus invade their space (Psalm 14:1; Romans 1:18–25). This unbelief can have multiple causes like fear, bad examples, bitterness, and misperceptions.

The doubt God consoles is *honest,* "Thomas-like" doubt. Jesus personally appeared to Thomas, quoted him, gave him hard evidence, and urged him to believe (John 20:26–27). Thomas' doubt was *not* a cover up for rebellion but a consequence of deep disappointment and misplaced expectations.

The Bible repeatedly uncovers God's consoling approach to non-rebellious doubters:

- With Job, God openly consoled him and rebuked his friends.

- David was comforted in his questioning of why God seemed to forsake him.
- Habakkuk was the prophet with a question mark for a mind, yet God reassured him.
- John the Baptist wondered in his imprisonment if Jesus was the Messiah, and Jesus responded by affirming his faith.
- Jesus healed the son of the father who cried, "I believe, help my unbelief!"

Honest doubt is part of a healthy and growing faith which learns to love God with the mind and adjust expectations with truth. The three who faced the fiery furnace expressed a healthy faith: "Our God, whom we serve, is able to deliver us . . . *but if not*, we are not going to serve your gods or worship the golden image" (Daniel 3:18). Thomas developed a "but if not" kind of faith. He would learn that Jesus defeated death by His resurrection, and thus he would see Jesus's death on the cross as good news. He saw the risen Christ again on the Sea of Galilee (John 21:2), was filled with the Holy Spirit at Pentecost (Acts 1:13), and tradition says he died for his faith in India. When doubt begins to disturb you, respond by first examining the cause: Is it rooted in rebellion or disappointment?[1]

Jesus had appeared to the other disciples without Thomas, and *eight days later*, Thomas joined them and declared his refusal to believe unless he had proof (John 20:24–26). So Thomas had spent some time alone with his doubts; he withdrew from the band of disciples, and his doubts grew worse. But when he returned to the fellowship, Jesus showed up and destroyed his doubts!

STAY IN THE FELLOWSHIP

This reveals the second habit we need to ingrain in our lives when we struggle: stay in the fellowship and be appropriately honest about our doubts.

What impressed me is that the other disciples did not exclude Thomas but welcomed him, doubts included. Jude, the half-brother of Jesus, later urged *us* to "have mercy on some who are doubting," like Jesus did with Thomas (Jude 1:22).

I have a long list of people who have come to a place of strong persevering faith in Christ after working through their doubts—sometimes over the course of many years—within our church family.

This can be hard for leaders to do, but refusing to stay in the fellowship and be honest about your "honest" doubts can end up damaging those who are looking to you for guidance. I have discovered I am often most effective when I share my "honest-doubt struggles" with my church family. It gives them permission to be honest, draws them in, and helps shape their view of Jesus as One Who consoles honest doubters.

EXAMINE THE EVIDENCE

As we examine how Jesus restored doubting Thomas, we learn a third habit we need to ingrain into our lives in response to honest doubt: examine the evidence.

Jesus appeared, greeted the disciples by saying, "Peace be with you," then turned to Thomas and gave him the evidence he'd insisted on in order to believe. In addition, Jesus gave Thomas His personal presence and assured him He'd been with Thomas in his doubts. Jesus actually quotes what Thomas said, as if to say, "I was there when you drew the line in the sand, and

I heard it all. I did not stop loving you then, and I am here now to give you the evidence you asked for. Your honest doubts did not push me away; they drew me closer to you."

Jesus did not condemn him; instead, he consoled him. The commands He gave Thomas are also consoling to us: get in touch with the evidence, and believe.

Faith always has an object, and the more evidence we acquire, the stronger our faith in it becomes (Romans 10:17). We cannot prove what we believe, but we can believe beyond a reasonable doubt, based on a solid trail of evidence.

We may be stuck in a place of unbelief because we have not seriously examined the evidence for ourselves. For example, many believe the Gospel accounts of the life, death, and resurrection of Jesus were written long after Jesus ascended to Heaven. However, the evidence reveals that the first accounts of the resurrection were not found in the four gospels but the thirteen books written by the apostle Paul. Even skeptical historians believe that Paul wrote them about fifteen to twenty years after the death of Christ. In 1 Corinthians 15:3–8, Paul writes,

> For I delivered to you as of first importance what I also received, that Christ died for our sins according to the Scriptures, and that He was buried, and that He was raised on the third day according to the Scriptures, and that He appeared to Cephas, then to the twelve. After that He appeared to more than five hundred brethren at one time, most of whom remain until now, but some have fallen asleep; then He appeared to James, then to all the apostles; and last of all, as to one untimely born, He appeared to me also.

Paul received the Gospel from Jesus directly, as Acts and Galatians make clear (Acts 9; Galatians 1–2). Yet, in 1 Corinthians 15:3–8, he declares that the gospel Paul received from Jesus and the gospel taught by the other apostles are the same.

Paul supports this by referring to the "creed" he quotes in 1 Corinthians 15:3–8. Liberal and conservative scholars agree that Paul is quoting a creed of the church's belief *before* Paul's conversion—the account of Christ's death and resurrection. Paul says he received that same revelation and cites Jesus's resurrection and specific appearances. This is solid evidence that the church believed in the bodily resurrection of Jesus from day one, and so did Paul and the authors of the four gospels. The accounts of the resurrection were not made up years after the event.

Refusing to examine the evidence can lead to cultural snobbery. It was *not* easier to believe in bodily resurrections in Jesus's day than in ours. British scholar N.T. Wright offers the latest and most extensive scholarship on Jesus's resurrection in his book *The Resurrection of the Son of God* (Fortress Press, 2003).[2] He provides an extensive survey of the beliefs of Jewish and non-Jewish people of the first-century Mediterranean world, both East and West. The universal view at that time was that bodily resurrection from the dead was *impossible.*

Greeks and Romans saw the soul or spirit as good and the body as weak and corrupt. To them, resurrection was not only impossible but undesirable. Their goal was to escape the vile body, not come back into it! The Jews believed in bodily resurrection for *all* the righteous in the last day, when God would renew the world and remove all suffering and death. Therefore, the idea of a single resurrection in the middle of history was unthinkable to them. The evidence tells us that people in Jesus's day were not any more likely to believe in His resurrection than we are today.

Thomas responded to the evidence Jesus gave him with an amazing statement: "My Lord and my God!" Here is a first-century Jew calling Jesus God! Jews believed worshiping man as God was utter blasphemy, and yet he is doing just that to

Jesus. The evidence shows us that after Jesus's death, His followers suddenly adopted a set of beliefs about Him rising again that were new and up to that point unthinkable.

Major worldview changes do not take place overnight. They normally occur in the context of dialogue, conflict, engagement, and exposure to new ideas over significant periods of time. Think how this has happened with slavery or the divine right of kings versus democracy. Yet the disciples experienced an *overnight, radical shift* in their worldview. They adopted a resurrection view of reality: They believed the future resurrection had already begun with Jesus. He had a new physical body, with scars on it to prove it was Him. He could eat, walk through walls, appear and disappear. His new resurrection body was a guarantee that His followers would one day also receive new resurrection bodies. They believed He was alive and living in them by the power of the Holy Spirit.

To them, the Passover meal was suddenly about Jesus. They gathered to worship on Sunday, the day He rose, even though all their lives they had set aside Saturday for worship. They considered the sacrifices, temple, and priesthood all fulfilled in Jesus. They now considered the unclean Gentiles who believed in Him as brothers and sisters in Christ.

Memorize these numbers: 12, 40, 8, 516+

Jesus appeared *twelve* times over a period of *forty* days in *eigh*t geographical locations at different times and to over *516* eyewitnesses.

Jesus gave Thomas and the listening disciples another beatitude: "Because you have seen Me, have you believed? *Blessed* are they who did not see, and yet believed" (John 20:29).

My scholarly wife was raised in the church, and Christianity was the only religion she had studied. She began to have honest doubts and wondered, "With nine thousand religions in the world, how do I know Christianity is the right one?"

She dealt with her doubts by examining the evidence. Her extensive two-year study helped her appreciate aspects of other faith traditions, but in the end, it strengthened her faith in the uniqueness of Jesus Christ and His claims to be the only way to God the Father.

Jesus's restoration of doubting Thomas demonstrates that honest doubt is part of a healthy faith. Doubt is an invitation to join Jesus in His work of strengthening our faith by examining the cause, staying in fellowship, and examining the evidence.

As a leader, ingrain these habits into your life and share openly your journey through doubt and disappointment with those you minister to. They need to know how you battle when DD invades your space!

All ministry leaders also need to know how to battle with FFC—*failures, fears,* and *comparisons.* Jesus's restoration of Peter tells us how to thrive and grow strong when these stalk us.

JESUS DEALS WITH PETER'S PAST FAILURES

So, when they had finished breakfast, Jesus said to Simon Peter, "Simon, son of John, do you love Me more than these?" He said to Him, "Yes, Lord; You know that I love You." He said to him, "Tend My lambs." He said to him again a second time, "Simon, son of John, do you love Me?" He said to Him, "Yes, Lord; You know that I love You." He said to him, "Shepherd My sheep." He said to him the third time, "Simon, son of John, do you love Me?" Peter was grieved because He said to him the third time, "Do you love Me?" And he said to Him, "Lord, you know all things; You know that I love You." Jesus said to him, "Tend My sheep. Truly, truly, I say to you, when you were younger, you used to gird yourself and walk wherever you wished; but when you grow old, you will stretch out your hands and someone else will gird you, and bring you where you do not wish to go." Now this He said, signifying by what kind of death he would glorify God. And when He had spoken this, He said to him, "Follow Me!" Peter, turning around, saw the disciple whom Jesus loved following them; the one who also had leaned back on His bosom at the supper and said, "Lord, who is the one who betrays You?" So Peter seeing him said to Jesus, "Lord, and what about this man?" Jesus said to him, "If I want him to remain until I come, what is that to you? You follow Me!" Therefore this saying went out among the brethren that that disciple would not die; yet Jesus did not say to him that he would not die, but only, "If I want him to remain until I come, what is that to you?" (John 21:15–23)

Just as Jesus restored Peter, so will He restore us. I know this because He is constantly praying for us and is on a quest to make us like Himself (Hebrews 7:25; Romans 8:28–29).

John 21 opens with an account of the third time Jesus appeared to His disciples after he was raised from the dead. Peter decided to go fishing on the Sea of Galilee, and six other disciples joined him. They fished all night and caught nothing until Jesus appeared on the shore and urged them to cast their net on the right-hand side of the boat. Then they caught 153 fish, and Peter jumped in the water, swam to shore, and pulled the catch in. Peter was greeted by Jesus, Who had a charcoal fire going with some fish on it and bread. The last time Peter had been near a charcoal fire was when he denied Jesus in the courtyard of the high priest. After breakfast, Jesus invited Peter to go on a walk with Him. We know this because John 21:20 says Peter saw John following them.

At first, it seems like Jesus is rubbing Peter's nose in his failures: The charcoal fire, three times addressing him as Simon (his name before Jesus changed it to Peter), and asking three times, "Do you love me?" Yet Jesus commissions him three times to care for His most prized possession, His people. As always, Jesus goes to the heart of the issue and fully restores Peter.

Jesus begins by asking him, "Simon, son of John, do you *love* me more than *these?*" Jesus uses the Greek word *agapao* for love. It is the same word used in John 3:16, which describes God's love for us, and is a word that means a self-sacrificing, unconditional love. Jesus added, "Do you *agapao* me more than *these?*" The reason Jesus added the term *these* is revealed in Jesus's prediction of Peter's denials. Matthew 26:33–35 and Mark 14:29–31 reveal that after the Passover meal, Jesus quoted Zechariah 13:7 and said it would be fulfilled by all his disciples forsaking him.

Peter then insisted, "Even though *all* (these other disciples) may fall away, I *never* will fall away!" Peter contradicted Jesus, challenged the word of God and put himself above the other disciples. Jesus then told Peter, "Truly, I say to you that this very night, before a rooster crows, you will deny Me three times." Peter responded by directly contradicting Jesus for a second time, insisting; "Even if I have to die with You, *I will not deny you!*" Peter is saying, "Lord, You don't know. *I* know!" Peter is putting all his faith in his own willpower as if he were saying to Jesus, "Now, Lord, you know this is Peter the rock you are talking about! You can relax and know this; all these *other* men may forsake you, but count on the rock, I never will!" Jesus wants to know if Peter is still thinking he knows better than Jesus, *comparing* himself to the other disciples and relying on his own will-power.

Peter's response to Jesus's question reveals a changed heart. He does not use the word *agapao* in response to Jesus's question but *phileo*, from which we get the word Philadelphia, which means brotherly love. The term means a warm affection, like that shared between friends. It is not the level of *agapao* love like a parent for a child. Peter says, "*Lord* (not Rabbi), *You* know (no longer I know), that *all I can say* is I have a 'warm affection' for you (not *agapao* love)." Peter is humble, dependent on Jesus's knowledge of him, and thus qualified to serve. So Jesus commissions him to care for His most prized possessions: His people, whom He calls His lambs.

Jesus questions Peter a second time. He again calls him Simon but removes the comparative ("these") and simply asks, "Simon, son of John, do you *agapao* me?" Peter responds by refusing to use *agapao* and repeats his humble response, "Yes Lord, you know that I *phileo* you." Jesus commissions him a second time, "Shepherd My sheep."

What is going on here? Jesus is replacing Peter's imbedded mental record of his failure with a focus on Jesus and His personal call on Peter's life. Echoes of this commission are revealed in Peter's two New Testament letters (1 Peter 5:1–5, 2 Peter 1:1–11).

Then, as if Jesus steps down from the high rung of the love ladder to stand on Peter's level at the base, He switches words. Jesus asks Peter the third time, "Simon, son of John" (not Peter) "do you *phileo* Me" (not *agapao* Me)—"Do you have a warm affection for Me?" Peter is grieved over the third question, as it must have reminded him of his three denials. This time, Peter adds a phrase in his response; "Lord, You know *all things*; You know I *phileo* love you." Jesus then re-commissions Peter the third time with, "Tend My sheep."

When our past failures shape our current reality, we need to do what Peter did: Come clean before Jesus about our arrogance, self-reliance, and comparisons, and put our full trust in Him. Peter's three-fold declaration of his own limited capacity for love and dependence on the full knowledge of Jesus was evidence of humble dependence and the qualification for effectively caring for God's people. Peter ended his exhortation to his fellow elders to shepherd the flock of God with a reminder of His unchanging nature: He is opposed to the proud but gives grace to the humble (1 Peter 5:5).

In one of his books, Henry Nouwen tells about the lesson of trust and faith he learned from a family of trapeze artists. He visited them after watching them "fly through the air with the greatest of ease" and asked one of the flyers his secret. The answer stuck with Nouwen and helped him understand better what it means to fully trust God: "The secret is that the flyer does nothing and the catcher does everything. When I fly to Joe, my catcher, I simply must stretch out my arms and hands and wait for him to catch me and pull me safely over the apron. The worst thing the flyer can do is try to catch the catcher. I am not supposed to catch Joe—it's Joe's job to catch me. If I grabbed Joe's wrists, I might break them, or he might break mine, and that would be the end of both of us. A flyer must fly, and a catcher must catch, and the flyer must trust, with out-stretched arms, that his catcher will be there for him."

That day on the shores of Galilee, Peter flew, and Jesus caught him. Jesus has never dropped anyone, and our failures teach us to trust Him with outstretched arms.

Jesus is not done with Peter. Put yourself in Peter's sandals: He had denied the Lord, he had been recommissioned by Jesus, and he had learned his lessons, but how did he know if he would stay on that path? How could he be confident he would not slip back to his old, self-confident patterns and disqualify himself? He must have had fears about his future!

JESUS DEALS WITH PETER'S FEARS ABOUT THE FUTURE

Jesus, the ever-wise shepherd and all-knowing one, pulls back the curtain on Peter's future and lets him have a peek! He tells

Peter two things: First, "You will live to an older age." No wonder when Peter was arrested in Jerusalem and his life was threatened, he slept like a baby (Acts 12:6). He was still young, and Jesus told him he would grow old. Second, Jesus told Peter of the death by which he would glorify God, as if to say, "Peter, you are going to finish well. I, the Chief Leak-Minder, will bring you through to the end!"

As Peter grew older, he wrote about what Jesus had told him regarding his future (2 Peter 1:12–15) and leveraged it to build God's people and glorify Him. Eusebius (AD 265–340), a Greek church father and historian, tells us that Peter and his wife were arrested under the reign of Nero and sentenced to death by crucifixion. Peter watched as they crucified his wife and kept telling her, "Remember our Lord." Peter ministered to his guards that night, and the next day, he was crucified. His last request, which was granted, was that he be crucified upside down, as he was not worthy of being crucified right-side up like his Lord.

Now you may think, "Jesus told Peter his future and held him fast to the end, but He has not done that for me." Oh, yes, He has! Philippians promises, "He who began a good work in you will perfect it until the day of Christ Jesus." Romans 8:28–29 must always be read with that in mind: "God causes *all things to work together for good* to those who love God, to those who are called according to His purpose. For those whom He foreknew, He also predestined *to become conformed to the image of His Son* . . ." The good which Jesus is working all things together for is that we be conformed into His likeness.

Jesus is on a quest, and He will fulfill His mission. He holds us and will mold us into His image and bring us safely home. Jesus ended his promise regarding Peter's future by commanding him, "Follow Me!"

JESUS DEALS WITH PETER'S BENT TO COMPARE

Consider what has happened to Peter. He is taking a walk with the risen Lord of the universe! Jesus is dealing with Peter's past failures and recommissioning him three times. Jesus pulls back the curtain of time and assures Peter of his future, which would end by glorifying God.

Peter, still a work in progress, like all of us, shifts his focus from Jesus to his friend John. "Lord what about this man?" It's as if to say, "You know, Lord, all this insider information about me is fascinating, so how about telling me John's future?"

Jesus immediately rebukes Peter and reminds him that He is in management and Peter is in sales! "If I want him to remain until I come, what is that to you? You follow Me!" In other words, "Stop comparing, focus on Me, and do what I have called *you* to do."

Comparisons are odious. They always steer us off the narrow path and usually into a ditch, where we end up feeling superior or inferior to others. This is a slow leak the Lord has had to mind and mend in me for years. How freeing to realize that our Shepherd has a unique path for each of us to follow, and we can only be the best *us* He designed us to be. Restoration from past failures, fears about our future, and our bent to compare is overcome by finding our adequacy in Jesus Christ.

Ministry leaders who learn to do battle with the DDFFC through faith in Christ don't lose heart.

Behind every "lose heart" circumstance is God's "strong heart" provision.

Did you know there are six "do not lose heart" passages in the New Testament? (Luke 18:1; 2 Corinthians 4:1, 16; Galatians

6:9; Ephesians 3:13; Hebrews 12:3; 2 Thessalonians 3:13). Read them this week, and you'll discover that, for every "lose heart" circumstance, God makes available a "strong heart" resource.

Biblically, losing heart is *not* discouragement, disappointment, fear, testing, fatigue, or frustration.

For example, before His arrest, Jesus was stressed to the point of sweating blood, three times pleaded with His disciples to pray for Him, and kept throwing Himself on the ground and repeatedly crying out to God (Hebrews 5:7, Matthew 26:36–46, Luke 22:39–46). Yet in all this, He did not lose heart. In addition, Paul was afflicted and despaired even of life (2 Corinthians 1:8–9). Yet he twice states that he did not lose heart during this season (2 Corinthians 4:1, 16).

Losing heart literally means to "give in to evil."

We lose heart when we cave into evil, both inside us and outside us, *by refusing to live by faith in the character and promises of God* (Hebrews 11:6). We stop looking to the author and perfecter of our faith, Jesus Christ, and we stop depending on the Holy Spirit (Hebrews 12:2; Galatians 5:16–26).

We do not *suddenly* lose heart. Losing heart is *always* preceded by unattended slow leaks in our walk with God. The leaks are often caused by the five dark horseman of the DDFFC! Praise God, we have all we need in Jesus Christ to plug the leaks and press on.

A HAPPY ENDING

Remember the mentor I told you about at the beginning of this book? The apparent "blow-out" in his life was preceded by a steady stream of unattended slow leaks. But the end of his story has been a source of great encouragement!

As I was writing this book and reflecting on his life, my wife asked me, "Have you ever considered checking to see how he is?" I am ashamed to admit that I was afraid to find out, but I eventually mustered my courage and did some research. I was elated with what I discovered! A series of articles in local newspapers about him showed me the faithfulness of God!

I connected with his family and confirmed the facts: My former mentor and his wife had been separated for seventeen years—but then they remarried each other! Their son, who is a pastor, conducted the wedding ceremony. My mentor is now in his 90s, loves the Lord, and spent several years serving as a chaplain. Our God never lets us go! He is the restorer of those who lose heart.

Yes, there is hope. Jesus Christ longs to instill His grace-sourced patterns in our lives, and they will plug our punctures and enable us to flourish. Our ultimate hope is in the grace of God, given to us by the author and perfecter of our faith, Jesus Christ (Hebrews 12:2).

"Minding the slow leaks" means to daily heed His grace-call. He is ever ready to teach you *the patterns* of grace which will empower you to flourish and finish well. Let's daily join Him in His work. He longs for us to flourish!

Workouts to Thrive and Finish Strong

1. Re-read the chapter, and outline the way Jesus restored Thomas and Peter. What insight was most helpful to you? Why? What steps can you take today to being to ingrain some of these restorative patterns in your life? Share what you have

learned with someone else and encourage each
other to instill these grace-sourced patterns into
your daily walk with God.

2. Compare the ways Jesus ministered to Thomas
   and Peter. Discover additional insights about how
   God restores us when we struggle with doubt and
   defeat. How did Jesus's approach to each differ?
   How were they the same? How do Thomas and
   Peter differ? How are they the same? Which one
   do you identify with the most? Why?

Thomas   John 20:24–29

Peter   John 21:15–23

3. Study the "do not lose heart" passages in the New
   Testament, and discover God's "strong heart" pro-
   visions behind every "lose heart" circumstance.
   (Luke 18:1; 2 Corinthians 4:1, 16; Galatians 6:9;
   Ephesians 3:13; Hebrews 12:3; 2 Thessalo-
   nians 3:13).

Passage	Circumstance	God's Provision
Luke 18:1–8		
2 Corinthians 4:1–18		
Galatians 6:6–10		
Ephesians 3:1–13		
Hebrews 12:1–3		
2 Thessalonians 3:6–13		

Notes

CHAPTER 1

1. J.D. Greear's excellent book, *Gospel: Recovering the Power That Made Christianity Revolutionary,* Chapter 10, "Expect Great Things," pages 161–175. Greear makes the concept of measuring God's compassion and power by the cross and resurrection very clear.
2. David Foster Wallace, "Top 10 Commencement Speeches of All Time."
3. John Piper's book *21 Servants of Sovereign Joy* (Crossway, 2018) is a great resource to discover how other leaders flourished by feeding their "faith filter."
4. For further elaboration on this point, I recommend Tim Keller's book *Preaching: Communicating Faith in an Age of Skepticism* (Viking, 2015), especially Chapter Three, "Preaching Christ From All of Scripture," pages 70–90.
5. John Piper's *God's Passion for His Glory: Living the Vision of Jonathan Edwards* (Crossway, 2006) clearly expounds this core biblical theme and its implications and explains how this truth shaped the life of Jonathan Edwards.
6. Packer, J. I. *The Plan of God.* Evangelical Press, 1965.

CHAPTER 2

1. "Josh Harris Is Kissing 'I Kissed Dating Goodbye' Goodbye," *Relevant Magazine,* Oct. 22, 2018.

2.   Several resources outline these movements, including *A Study of Denominations* by Ethan R. Longhenry and *The American Evangelical Story: A History of the Movement* by Douglas A. Sweeney.

3.   Together for the Gospel and The Gospel Coalition are two frontrunners in this movement.

4.   "The Four-Fold Praise" is a tool that will help you from the moment you wake up. For over twenty years, I have found this simple spiritual disciple to be a primary source of thriving and staying strong in the Lord. I challenge you to use it every day for a week. I think you might get hooked if you do. It is provided in the appendix. Use it and pass it on to others.

5.   "The Gospel U" is a very helpful, tried and tested tool which will help you personally apply the Gospel to the heart of your issues and enable you to equip others to do the same. It is provided in the appendix. Use it and pass it along!

6.   I recommend The Five Solas Series by Thomas R. Schreiner, David VanDrunen, and Matthew Barrett. I read these for a series on the Five Solas during the 500th celebration of the Reformation.

7.   I have included in the appendix two simple ways to teach the storyline of the Bible—a one-minute overview and a ten-minute overview. These can be used effectively for evangelism and discipleship. Many believers know Bible stories and concepts but have not learned first how the whole story fits together to present the Gospel. If we do not first understand who Jesus is and what He came to do, we do not understand salvation or the Bible's message.

8.   The second section of The Four-Fold Praise: Praise God for Who You Are in Christ (appendix) is a good way to daily review this important truth.

9.   Tim Keller's book *Preaching: Communicating Faith in the Age of Skepticism* (Penguin Random House, 2015) is an excellent resource for every Gospel preacher.

10.   Two helpful resources on racial reconciliation which keep the Gospel central are *Heal Us, Emmanuel: A Call for Racial Reconciliation* (White Blackbird Books, 2016) by thirty church leaders and General Editor Doug Serven and *The Minority Experience: Navigating Emotional and Organizational Realities* by Adrian Pei (IVP Books, 2018).

CHAPTER 3

1.   *Canals of Mars* by the editors of Encyclopedia Britannica https://www.britannica.com; *Percival Lowell and the History of Mars*, Robert Crossley. *The Massachusetts Review* Vol. 41, No. 3 (Autumn 2000).

2.   Jesus obviously works through sinful people, not just those who have placed their faith in Christ. Jesus told Pilate, "You would have no authority over me unless it was given to you from above; for this reason, he who delivered Me to you have the greater sin" (John 19:11). Peter declared that Jesus was delivered up by the predetermined plan and foreknowledge of God and added that He was "nailed to a cross by the hands of godless men" (Luke 22:22). Jesus came to seek and save the lost, and He claimed to have all authority in Heaven and on earth (Luke 19:1, Matthew 28:18). He fulfilled these purposes through *both* the saved and the lost.

3.   Jesus *directly* works through those who know Him by faith. Ephesians 2:10 says we are His workmanship and created for good works that God prepared beforehand so that we should walk in them. Colossians 3:23 urges all believers to work heartily in whatever they do; as the Reformers taught, all legitimate callings are sacred callings. We are commanded to do all for the glory of God in 1 Corinthians 10:31.

4.   See Appendix, "A Team of Elders with a Lead Pastor." This will help you think through the biblical priority of a team of qualified shepherds with a leader overseeing a local church. Explore the difference between a leader with a team and a team with a leader.

CHAPTER 4

1.   I was preaching on Titus 3 and focused on verse seven: "Being *justified by His grace* we would be made heirs according to the hope of eternal life."

2.   *The Secret Thoughts of an Unlikely Convert: An English Professor's Journey into Christian Faith* by Rosaria Champagne Butterfield (Crown & Covenant Publications, 2012).

3.   *Same-Sex Attraction and the Church: The Surprising Plausibility of the Celibate Life* by Ed Shaw (InterVarsity Press, 2015).

4.   *Susan and Anna Warner* by Edward Halsey Foster (Twayne Publishers, 1978).

CHAPTER 5

1.   There is a grove of Giant Sequoia trees in the southern part of Yosemite National Park. Some trees are over two hundred feet high and others have a circumference of ninety-two feet. In this grove is The Faithful Couple: two trees grew so close that their trunks fused at the base. Just as many have walked by the Faithful Couple and been inspired so, God longs for your marriage to be one that inspires generations. Imagine generations saying, "Now there is a faithful couple!

    Not far from The Faithful Couple are two streams that have merged. At the point where they come together, the water is turbulent and difficult to cross. But downstream, the water runs deep, the current is smooth, and it supports an abundance of marine life. Marriage often begins like those streams: At first, the two seeking to become one face many clashes, and the waters of marriage can be turbulent. As time passes and covenant love grows, the turbulence ceases and is replaced by deep bonds of unity, united strength, and birth of a life that flourishes in the flow of marital intimacy.

2.   "Keep the Home-Fires Burning" was a British patriotic First World War song composed in 1914 by Ivor Novello with words by Lena Guilbert Ford.

3.   Peter Scazzero's book, *The Emotionally Healthy Church* (Zondervan, 2005) has been a treasure chest of truth for me.

4.   See instructions for "The Marriage Box" in the appendix. I promise, if you do this, you will remember God's definition of marriage and be able to pass it on to others, decades after doing the exercise. Teach it to your children and to those you lead!

5.   I urge you to read the well-researched book by Shaunti Feldhahn *The Good News about Marriage: Debunking Discouraging Myths About Marriage* (Multnomah, 2014).

6.   To download a personal guide to writing a tribute, order the book *The Best Gift You Can Ever Give Your Parents,* or to see examples of others' tributes, visit www.familylife.com/tribute.

CHAPTER 6

1. Biography of the life of Johnathan Edwards, by Jason Meyer—2019 Bethlehem Conference for Pastors. I also highly recommend John Piper's book, *21 Servants of Sovereign Joy: Faithful, Flawed and Fruitful* (Crossway, 2018).
2. Antipas divorced his wife, Phasaelis, and married his half-brother's wife, Herodias. John the Baptist condemned the unlawful marriage and was arrested and eventually beheaded.
3. Antipas was accused of conspiracy against emperor Caligula and exiled to Gaul, where he died.
4. *Meet Your Conscience* by Warren Wiersbe (Compass House Publishers, 1985).

CHAPTER 7

1. Proverbs identifies over thirty different kinds of people and tells us how to wisely relate to each. It also instructs us in how to be wise and avoid the path of foolishness. Learning to respond to criticism by the grace of God is foundational to living a wise life. An article every leader should have in their file and review often is "The Cross and Criticism" by Alfred Poirier (https://faculty.wts.edu/wp-content/uploads/2018/04/The-Cross-and-Criticism-Alfred-J.-Poirier.pdf).

CHAPTER 8

1. A book that helped me clarify the difference between honest doubt and rebellion is *Disappointment with God* by Philip Yancey (Zondervan, 1988). He traces the unusual theme of disappointment with God through the Bible and provides some helpful insights on the reality of living by faith.
2. *The Resurrection of the Son of God* by N.T. Wright (Fortress Press, 2003), pages 32–200.

The Gospel U

The Gospel U is a tool which our team of pastors developed as we learned together how to let the Gospel shape our lives. We have found it to be an effective way to communicate how the process works. I urge you to master the concept, practice sharing it with other believers, and weave it into your own teaching ministry.

My wife, Mae Belle, dubbed this tool "The Gospel U" while we were discussing the concepts. We begin by drawing a U in the center of a piece of paper or a white board. The U reminds us that this is about YOU and your relationship with Christ.

Note that we have placed four blanks around the U. On the top left is the word Issues. We all have issues! Worry, stress, people who irritate us, fears, addictions, insecurities, pride, etc.

Most of us seek to deal with our issues by making a change in our behavior. This is important and often produces beneficial results. However, lasting change is rooted in something deeper. Focusing only on behavior modification is a common trap that ignores the underlying root causes of our issues.

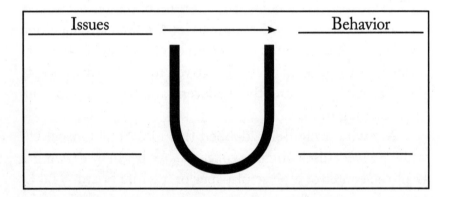

Dealing with our issues only by changing our behavior can lead to two negative, self-defeating attitudes. One is pride. We begin to build our identity and significance around our positive behavior, slowly begin to rely on our willpower and disciplines as our "saviors," and grow overconfident. When we compare ourselves to others who are unable to make the same changes we have, we see ourselves as superior. New mindsets begin to take root, like "winners never quit, and quitters never win." We believe we are winners because of our change in behavior. We can become "little Pharisees" who in our hearts agree with the man who went up to the temple to pray, *"Lord, I thank you that I am not like other people; swindlers, unjust, adulterers, or even like this tax collector"* (Luke 18:9–14). A change in behavior, rooted in self-effort, can lead to an attitude of pride.

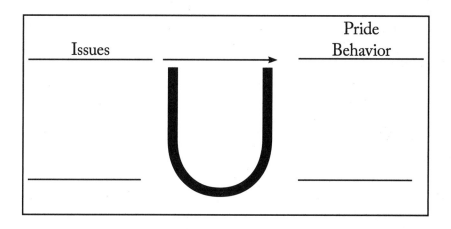

The other self-defeating attitude is to fall into the "pit" of despair. We put disciplines into our lives, make ourselves accountable, and our behavior changes—but we still experience relapses and failures. Because our hope is rooted in our resolve, we hide our failures and live with frustration and guilt. We begin to believe the lie that we earn God's approval by our behavior, not by faith in the work of Christ. This belief feeds insecurity and pushes us to try harder. Our heart cry resembles the one Paul uttered in Romans 7:24: *"Wretched man that I am! Who will set me free from the body of this death!"*

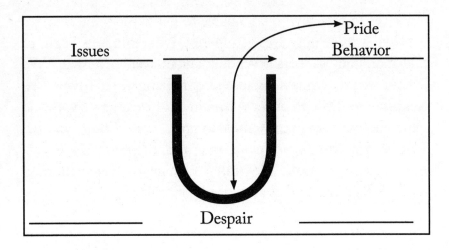

Many of us live our "Christian" lives like yo-yos, bouncing back and forth between pride and despair. This cycle gradually shapes our view of God and ourselves, and we adopt a Jesus-plus approach to salvation. We focus on ourselves and do our best to earn God's approval. We begin to see Christianity as primarily a self-improvement program and behavior-modification process. Our hope is not in the work of Jesus Christ on our behalf but in our own willpower and resolve.

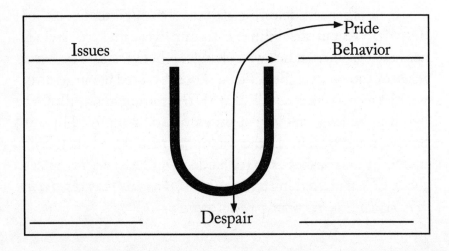

Viewing Christianity as primarily a change in behavior, rooted in human resolve, is a man-centered, anti-grace approach to salvation. It produces both self-deceived, prideful Pharisees and defeated, shame-filled people. It is a "surface level" approach to Christianity because it does not put the Gospel in the center and it overlooks the underlying root causes of our issues.

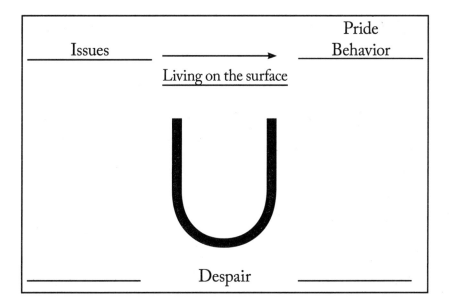

God has a better way—the Good News, heart-changing Gospel way! Jesus did not come just to be an example for us to try to imitate by willpower. Jesus did not die to make bad people good but to make spiritually dead people alive (Ephesians 2:1–10). God always goes below the surface and works to bring about lasting *heart* change.

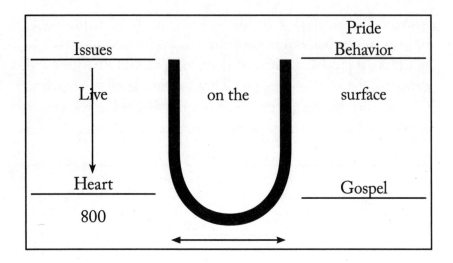

THE HEART OF EVERY ISSUE IS THE ISSUE OF THE HEART

Did you know the word *heart* is found in the Bible eight hundred times? I would call that a major theme! God always targets our heart because the heart of every issue is the issue of the heart.

- Proverbs 4:23 warns, "Watch over your *heart* with all diligence, for from it flow the springs of life."
- Paul reminded Timothy of the target he was to aim at every time he taught the word of God: "The goal of our instruction is love from a pure *heart* and a good conscience and a sincere faith."

Biblically speaking, the heart represents the core of our being, the source of our hopes, identity, and purpose. It is directly tied to our motives. Jesus taught that our heart always has a treasure (Matthew 6:21). He explained that our words reveal the treasure of our heart: *"What comes out of the mouth fills the heart"* (Matthew 15:15–20). Calvin declared that the heart is an idol factory, which means we are worshipers by nature and we all cling to little saviors and lords to find security and significance. Our "idol factory" hearts take good things and turn them into *god* things.

The problem is that we do not have the power to change our hearts! Willpower, accountability, resolutions, disciplines, positive mental attitudes, religious disciplines, and perseverance will not change the bent of our heart. The prophet Jeremiah said, "The heart is more deceitful than all else and desperately sick; who can understand it?" (Jeremiah 17:9).

The *only* power that can change the heart is the Gospel of Jesus Christ (2 Corinthians 5:17). God promises believers a new heart when we place our faith in Jesus Christ for salvation (Ezekiel 36:26, John 3:3, John 7:38–39, Colossians 1:13–14). Paul described salvation this way: "You turned to God from idols to serve a living and true God," which is an apt description of heart change (1 Thessalonians 1:9). We must learn how to habitually, by faith, experience a heart-Gospel interchange to experience lasting change.

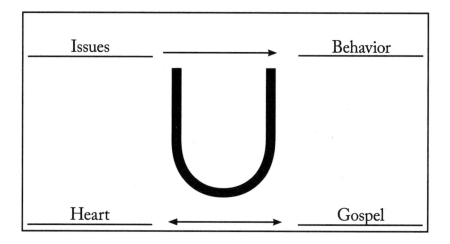

When we trust in Jesus Christ for salvation, not only do we receive a new heart, we are given a new identity in Christ and receive a new power by the Holy Spirit (2 Corinthians 5:17, John 7:37–38). God wants our behavior to be shaped by a heart-Gospel interchange, which reflects our union with Christ and the power of the Holy Spirit. Our new identity in Christ is to be reflected in our behavior: We are to love as we have been loved (Romans 5:5), to forgive as we have been forgiven (Ephesians 4:32), to pray for others as Christ is constantly praying for us (Hebrews 7:25), to live pure lives as temples of the Holy Spirit (1 Corinthians 6:19–20), etc. God wants the change in our behavior to come *from* our hearts as we continually apply the Gospel to every aspect of our lives. God's way of changing us is to go *below the surface* and change our hearts by the Gospel, which leads to a change in our behavior.

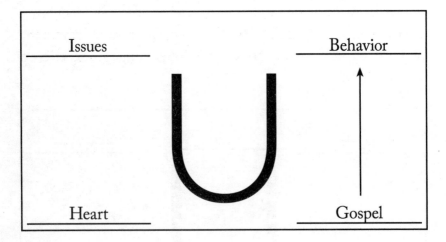

The Gospel U helps us understand how to put Gospel patterns into our lives that will help us finish well. What does it look like to apply the Gospel to the issues of our lives so that we experience a heart and behavior change?

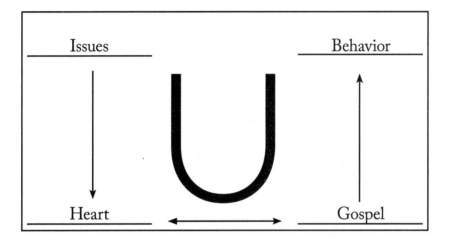

The Four-Fold Praise

"Through Him then, let us continually offer up a sacrifice of praise to God, that is the fruit of lips that give thanks to His name."

—Hebrews 13:15

"If anyone loves Me, he will keep My word; and My Father will love him, and we will come to him and make Our abode with him."

—John 14:23

PRAISE GOD FOR WHO HE IS.

"Delight yourself in the LORD; And He will give you the desires of your heart." (Psalm 37:4)

GOD'S MORAL ATTRIBUTES

Some have called these God's communicable attributes because we, being made in His image, can imitate them. "Therefore, be imitators of God, as beloved children; and walk in love, just as Christ also loved you and gave Himself up for us, an offering and a sacrifice to God as a fragrant aroma" (Ephesians 5:1–2).

Love	Gentleness	Wrath
Joy	Self-control	Mercy
Peace	Benevolence	Truthfulness
Patience	Graciousness	Righteousness
Kindness	Holiness	Wisdom
Goodness	Jealousy	Discernment
Faithfulness	Justice	Beauty

GOD'S NATURAL ATTRIBUTES

God's incommunicable attributes are those that belong to Him alone. "I am the LORD, and there is no other; Besides Me there is no God" Isaiah 45:5. "To whom would you liken Me and make Me equal and compare Me, that we would be alike?" Isaiah 46:5. "I am the LORD, that is My name; I will not give My glory to another" (Isaiah 42:8).

All-knowing	Immanent	Self-existent
All-wise	Immutable	Self-sufficient
All-powerful	Independent	Sovereign
Creator	Judge	Transcendent
Eternal	Omnipresent	Triune
Incomprehensible	Majestic	
Infinite	Perfect	

PRAISE GOD FOR WHO YOU ARE IN CHRIST.

But by His doing you are in Christ Jesus, who became to us wisdom from God, and righteousness and sanctification, and redemption, so that just as it is written, "Let Him who boasts boast in the Lord." (1 Corinthians 1:30–31.)

All the moral and ethical commands given to believers are rooted in, based on, and shaped by our union with Jesus. The phrases "in Christ," "in Him," and "in the Lord" are used over 160 times in the New Testament. Being in Christ is not like being tools in a box or clothes in a closet; it's being like a branch in a vine or a limb in a body. A survey of the "in Christ" passages reveal over forty truths about our identity in the Lord. Only twenty are provided here. Begin each day by praising God for who He has made you in Christ, then act like it in the power of the Holy Spirit.

Know who you are in Christ	Act like who you are in Christ
Alive to God	*Live the life*
Ephesians 2:4–5, Colossians 3:1–4	Ephesians 4:1–2, Colossians 3:5–11
Loved	*Love*
1 John 4:10, Romans 5:8	Romans 5:5, Ephesians 5:1–2
Dead to sin	*Give no place to sin*
Romans 6:2–10	Romans 6:11–15
Forgiven	*Forgive*
Ephesians 1:7, Colossians 1:13–14	Ephesians 4:32; Romans 8:1, 33–34
Righteous	*Live righteously*
Philippians 3:9, Galatians 2:16	Philippians 3:13–14, Galatians 2:20

Child of God	***Act like His child***
John 1:12–13	Ephesians 5:1, 1 Peter 1:14–15
God's possession	***Yield to God***
2 Timothy 2:19, 1 Peter 1:18	Romans 12:1–2, 2 Timothy 2:19–21
Heir of God	***Add to your inheritance***
Romans 8:17, Colossians 1:12, Ephesians 1:11	Matthew 6:19–21, 2 Corinthians 5:9–10
Possessor of every spiritual blessing	***Seek things above***
Ephesians 1:3, 2:6; 2 Peter 1:3–4	Colossians 3:1–2
Blessed by God	***Give a blessing***
1 Peter 3:9–12	1 Peter 3:8–9
Servant of God	***Serve***
1 Corinthians 7:22–23, Romans 6:22	Romans 6:17–19, 12:11; Hebrews 12:28
New creation in Christ	***Walk in newness of life***
2 Corinthians 5:17	Romans 6:4
Free from the law	***Live in Christ***
Romans 6:14; 7:1–6	Galatians 5:1, Romans 8:4
Light of the world	***Let your light shine***
1 Thessalonians 5:5, Matthew 5:14	Ephesians 5:8, Matthew 5:15–16
Victorious over Satan	***Claim your victory***
Revelation 12:9–11, Colossians 1:13–14	Ephesians 6:11–17, James 4:7
Cleansed	***Live a clean life***
John 15:3; 1 John 1:7, 9	2 Corinthians 7:1, Philemon 4:8
Possessor of peace	***Be a peacemaker***
Romans 5:1, 14:17; John 14:27	Romans 12:18, 14:19; Colossians 3:15

Received God's grace	*Grow in grace*
Ephesians 2:8–9	2 Peter 3:18
Indwelt by the Holy Spirit	*Yield to the Holy Spirit*
1 Corinthians 6:19–20,	Ephesians 5:18, 4:30;
Romans 8:9, 14	1 Thessalonians 5:19
Spiritual gifts	*Use your gift*
1 Corinthians 12:4–13,	Romans 12:6–8,
Romans 12:3–6	1 Peter 4:10–11

PRAISE GOD FOR THE HOLY SPIRIT, AND INVITE HIM TO FULFILL HIS "JOB DESCRIPTION" IN YOU.

The Holy Spirit is God, the third person of the Trinity, and your source of power in the Christian life. Daily review his divine "job description," which covers every aspect of your life. Learn to cooperate with the Holy Spirit, Who is on duty constantly and eager to empower you.

1. Convicts of sin, righteousness, and judgment (John 16:7–11)
2. Glorifies Jesus Christ (John 16:14)
3. Regenerates us (Titus 3:5, John 3:5, 8)
4. Baptized with (1 Corinthians 12:13)
5. Sealed with (Ephesians 1:13, 4:30)
6. Indwelt with (1 Corinthians 6:19–20)
7. Anointed with (1 John 2:20, 27)
8. Gives assurance of salvation (Romans 8:14–16)
9. Fills, controls, and empowers us (Ephesians 5:17–21)
10. Leads us (Romans 8:14)
11. Imparts spiritual gifts to us (1 Corinthians 12:7, 11)

12. Illuminates Scripture to the believer (John 14:26, 16:12–15;1 Corinthians 2:12–16; 1 John 2:20, 27)
13. Intercedes for us (Romans 8:26)
14. Produces Christlike character in us (John 7:38–39, Galatians 5:22–23)
15. Gives us the power to love (Romans 5:5)
16. Sanctifies us (1 Peter 1:2)
17. Transforms us into the image of Jesus (2 Corinthians 3:18, 1 Corinthians 6:11)
18. Empowers us to witness of Christ (Acts 1:8)
19. Comforts and counsels us (John 14:16, 2 Corinthians 1:3–5)
20. Will raise and transform our bodies (Romans 8:11)

PRAISE GOD FOR THE ARMOR HE PROVIDES, AND PUT IT ON BY FAITH

But put on the Lord Jesus Christ and make no provision for the flesh in regard to its lusts. (Romans 13:14)

Ephesians 6:10–20:

- Gird your loins with truth
- Put on the breastplate of righteousness
- Shod your feet with the preparation of the Gospel
- Take up the shield of faith
- Put on the helmet of salvation
- Take up the sword of the Spirit

Now bring your request to God!

Therefore, let us draw near with confidence to the throne of grace, so that we may receive mercy and find grace to help in time of need. (Hebrews 4:16)

The 32/18 Principle from Hebrews

D o you treasure Jesus Christ above all else? A careful reading of Hebrews unveils The 32/18 Principle: Thirty-two joys that accompany treasuring Christ, and eighteen sorrows that accompany unbelief.

32 JOYS THAT ACCOMPANY TREASURING CHRIST

2:18   Jesus Christ comes to your aid when you are tempted.

3:6   You have confidence and hope because you are "owned" by Jesus.

3:13   You escape being hardened and deceived by sin, and you develop healthy relationships with other believers.

3:14   You partake of Christ, hold fast to your assurance in Him, and never give up.

4:3   You experience God's rest in your soul.

4:16   You experience the nearness of God and receive mercy and grace in your time of need.

5:14   You are trained to discern between good and evil. Discernment and wisdom are yours.

6:10   Your ministry to others will be fruitful and remembered by God.

6:12   You will have faith and patience so that you inherit the promises of God.

6:18   Jesus Christ is your refuge, your source of encouragement, and your hope.

7:19   You have a better hope in Jesus than in any other source, and you daily draw near to God.

7:25   You experience assurance of salvation, draw near to God, and rest in the knowledge that Christ is praying for you.

9:14   Your conscience is clean, and you serve the living God.

10:19   You have confidence to enter the presence of God by the blood of Jesus.

10:22   You draw near to God with a true heart and full assurance of faith because your conscience is clean before Him.

10:25   You are habitually encouraged by other believers and confident that Christ is coming back.

10:34   Things do not own you; you know you have lasting treasure in Heaven.

10:35   Your confidence in God will have a great reward.

11:1   You have assurance of things hoped for and a strong conviction of things not seen.

11:5   You are pleasing to God, and you will be taken home to Him when you die.

11:16   God is not ashamed to be called your God, and He has prepared a place for you in Heaven.

11:26   You consider the reproach of Christ better riches than what the world offers, and you are confident of your heavenly reward.

11:39   You gain approval before God because of faith in Him.

12:3   You daily consider Jesus and do not lose heart.

12:10   You know that God's discipline is for your own good.

12:11   You are trained by God's discipline and you reap wonderful benefits because of what He does in you.

12:14   You pursue peace with all people, and you are set apart by God for His purposes.

12:28   You will receive a kingdom that cannot be shaken, and your daily life is marked by gratitude to God.

13:5   Your character is free from the love of money. You are content with what you have, and you know that God will never forsake you.

13:9   You are not carried away by lies, but your heart is daily strengthened by God's grace.

13:17   You know how to properly submit to godly spiritual leaders, which results in their joy and your growth.

13:21   You are equipped by God to fulfill your purpose in life and have confidence that God is working in and through you.

18 SORROWS THAT ACCOMPANY UNBELIEF

2:1   You have drifted away from God and no longer hear His voice.

2:3   You are reaping the consequences of neglecting your salvation.

3:12   Your heart is evil and full of unbelief; you have walked away from the Living God.

3:13   You are hardened by sin and deceived.

4:1   You daily miss out on the rest God has for you in Christ.

4:11   You live in a barren "wilderness of unbelief."

5:11   You can't hear God's voice or understand His truth.

5:12   You are a spiritual baby and can only drink spiritual milk; you would choke on healthy truth!

6:8   Your life is close to being cursed; it bears no fruit and is wasted.

6:12   You give up on God and His promises and never experience the joy of believing Him.

10:27   You can count on a terrifying judgment from God because of your willful unbelief.

10:29   You can expect a severe punishment from God for your rebellion and unbelief.

12:5   You do not learn wisdom from the hard things God puts in your life.

12:15   You only want God's grace for yourself; you will not forgive those who wrong you, and you pollute the family of God.

12:25   You refuse to hear God, and then you get mad when He disciplines you for not listening to Him.

13:5   You love money and never experience contentment.

13:17   You are a pain in the neck to godly church leaders, and you miss out on what God wants to give you through them.

13:21   You are not equipped to do God's will and are wasting your life.

APPENDIX 4

The Marriage Box

A creative way to remember and celebrate with others God's definition of marriage is to make a "marriage box" together. It is a project we give to couples who go through our premarital counseling ministry.

First find a gift box, which symbolizes receiving your mate as a gift from God. I have seen many creative gift boxes through the years—wood, glass, paper—all decorated to represent a gift.

Second, place a pine cone in the box. Just as the pine cone must leave the tree before it can go into the ground and form a new tree, so we must leave father and mother before we can bond with our mate and form a new union.

Third, place a small bottle of glue in the box; this stands for cleaving unto your mate. The Hebrew word translated "be joined to" or "cleave unto" your mate in Genesis 2:24 literally means "to be glued together." We need to habitually renew our commitment to each other and not pour acids on the glue of our covenant vow.

Fourth, place a triangle in the box. This represents becoming one flesh. If you picture God at the top of the triangle and husband and wife on each of the bases, then as they move up the base toward God, they also move closer to each other. When God is the focal point of marriage, the benefits of one relationship with Him bless your relationship.

Fifth, place a pair of glasses or something else that is transparent into the box. This represents the husband and wife being "naked and not ashamed." It is a visual reminder of the importance of transparency in marriage.

Many couples place their "marriage box" on their mantel or on a prominent shelf in their home as a daily reminder of God's definition of marriage. I have heard many stories of couples sharing the definition of marriage with others because they asked about the meaning of the box on the shelf. The marriage box opens doors for Gospel conservations and interactions about the true meaning of marriage.

A Team of Elders with a Lead Pastor

A LEADER WITH A TEAM

Our church family has a long history of following the model of *a leader with a team*—a senior pastor, as *leader, with a team* of deacons and staff *who assist him* in overseeing and shepherding the flock. Over the last twenty years, we have modified this model to a senior pastor, as *leader, with a team* of pastors and deacons, *who assist him* in overseeing and shepherding the flock.

A TEAM WITH A LEADER

After a careful study of the Scriptures, we moved to a model of *a team with a leader:* A senior pastor, *as leader, with a team* of pastors and elders, *who together* oversee and shepherd the flock and are assisted by deacons.

Now we are seeking to better align ourselves with this new structure. We do not see past models as unbiblical, but we do see our model as a healthy one supported by Scripture. The title of "lead pastor," instead of "senior pastor," reflects our mindset.

LEADER/TEAM BALANCE

Any organization needs leadership. Healthy organizations have a leader who models effective teamwork with other leaders. A healthy balance of *a team with a leader* is revealed in the New Testament. This avoids the extremes of a "teamless leader" or a "leaderless team." We see this in the ministries of Jesus, Paul, Peter, John, James, Timothy, Titus, and Jude: a healthy team with a leader.

In addition, local churches in the New Testament were led by teams of elders but often a key leader would emerge (Acts 2:14; 3:12; 4:8; 5:3; 11:4; 12:2–3; 13:2, 9, 13, 16; 15:7, 13–22; 1 Corinthians 1:1; 16:10, 12; 1 Timothy 1:2–5; 6:20; 2 Timothy 1:2; 4:19–22; Titus 1:4–5; 3:12–14). Local churches need both a leader and a team of leaders to shepherd the flock. The New Testament refers to both leader and team as elders, overseers/ bishops, and pastors (Acts 20:17–38; Ephesians 4:11–14; 1 Timothy 3:1–7; Titus 1:5–9; Hebrews 13:7, 17; James 5:14; 1 Peter 5:1–5).

Those who favor a *hierarchal structure* tend to downplay Scriptures that support servant leadership, team work among elders, or the dangers of concentrated authority in one person. Too much emphasis on rank can foster leadership by position instead of leadership by influence and diminish each elder's call and the need for accountability to fulfill that call. Jesus, Peter, and John all warned against a "big-me, little-you," "lording-it-over" spirit in spiritual leaders and insisted that Christ-like servant leadership be the hallmark of leaders representing Jesus

Christ (Matthew 20:24–28, Luke 22:24–27, 1 Peter 5:3, 3 John 9–10).

Those who favor a *flat structure* tend to downplay Scriptures that support a team leader as well as the functional aspects of healthy organizations needing a leader. Too much emphasis on *equal roles* can downplay the need for the *role of a leader of the team* and accountability of team members. Peter leads by exhorting his fellow elders and young men in the flock, reminding them of their joint tasks and accountability to the Chief Shepherd Jesus Christ (1 Peter 1:1, 5:1–6).

In addition, he writes to scattered and persecuted believes, urging them to remember God's Word spoken by the prophets and the commands of Jesus, spoken by the apostles (2 Peter 1:1, 3:1–2). Paul, with Timothy his co-laborer, leads by writing to a fellow worker appealing to him to apply the Gospel to his relationship with his former servant (Philemon 1:1–3). John, referring to himself as the elder, leads by writing to encourage and shepherd his spiritual children in the Gospel (1 John 1:1, 2:1, 5:21, 2 John 1:1, 3 John 1:1). Jude, a bondservant of Jesus Christ, leads by writing to his fellow believers, urging them to content earnestly for the faith (James 1:1–4). Paul, the obvious servant leader, on his missionary journeys, eagerly equips and multiplies other leaders (Acts 13–20, 2 Timothy 2:2). Paul wrote his letters to Timothy, not all the elders of the church in Ephesus, and Titus, not others on his team. In each case, Paul assigned specific leadership responsibilities to Timothy and Titus that he did not assign to other elders (1 Timothy 1:3; 4:6, 11; 6:2; 2 Timothy 4:1–2; Titus 1:5–9; 2–3).

In our attempts to model healthy servant leadership, we must avoid swinging to extremes. We should not foster a *hierarchical "teamless leader"* mindset, which leads to too much power in one man, a lack of gift balance in leadership, and unhealthy shepherding of God's flock. Nor should we foster a *flat "leaderless team" structure*, which breeds confusion, power struggles, and insecurity. We favor an approach based on *a team of elders with a leader.*

ELDER COUNCIL

We believe a healthy, biblically based pattern of leadership in the local church consists of elders and deacons (Philippians 1:1, 1 Timothy 3:1–13, Titus 1:5–9). Elders are mature in Christ, oversee the work of the ministry, and shepherd the flock of God (Acts 20:17, 28–32; 1 Peter 5:1–5; 1 Timothy 3:1–7; Titus 1:5–9). Elders are biblically qualified, vetted by the Elder Council, and recommended to and affirmed by the church family. The Elder Council consists of all full-time vocational pastors, along with lay elders. The council has at least one more lay elder than full-time vocational pastors. The Chair, Vice-Chair, and Secretary of the council are lay elders. The lead pastor and associate pastors fulfill their roles as outlined in their job descriptions. Deacons serve under the leadership of the elders and care for the practical needs of the church family (Acts 6:1–7, 1 Timothy 3:8–13). Deacons are biblically qualified, vetted by the elders, and recommended to and affirmed by the church family.

As we hold to *a team with a leader* mindset, we have a Lead Pastor position. Both the team and the leader are intentionally accountable to one another and the flock of God. They are functionally shaped by the Gospel, which demands mutual submission, teamwork, accountability, service, and love.

Models of this healthy approach are woven through the New Testament. The Jerusalem Council brought together elders and apostles to settle a doctrine dispute. Key leaders Peter,

Barnabas, Paul, and James emerged and led by persuasion. James made an appeal that the apostles, elders, and church supported and implemented with a team of godly representatives (Acts 15).

Paul exhorted his fellow elders to serve sacrificially, and he led by example (Acts 20:13–38). Paul charged the Corinthian church to regard their leaders as servants of Christ and stewards (i.e., managers not owners) of the mysteries of God. Paul publicly confronted his fellow elders, Peter and Barnabas, when they were not straightforward about the truth of the Gospel (Galatians 2:11–14). Paul writes two books to his understudy and fellow elder, Timothy (1 and 2 Timothy). He instructed him on how to conduct himself in the household of God, the church of the living God. Timothy's leadership included equipping and leading the church and other elders as well as deacons (*elders*: 1 Timothy 1:3–7, 3:1–13, 4:1–16, 5:17–25, 6:20–21, 2 Timothy 1:1–4:22, *the church*: 1 Timothy 2:1–15, 3:14–16, 5:1–16, 6:1–19, 2 Timothy 4:11–16, 5:17–22).

LEAD PASTOR AND ASSOCIATE PASTORS

The lead pastor on a team of elders is called to be a servant leader. He is accountable to his fellow elders to fulfill his role in humility as he leans on the gifts of his co-laborers and fosters teamwork and healthy oversight of the flock of God. He is to lead, feed, and shepherd those allotted to their charge *with* the team of elders. He is to assume primary responsibility for providing Christ-centered preaching of the whole counsel of God at all regular services of the church. He leads by example as he feeds the flock with God's word, shepherds God's people, does the work of an evangelist, and casts vision to connect God's people to God's purposes.

Associate pastors and lay elders are to be held accountable to live within biblical guardrails. All elders have an equal voice on the Elder Council, and all associate pastors are elders. Associate pastors are to be accountable to the lead pastor and/or his designate as well as to the elder council. They are to fulfill their assigned roles with direct oversight from the lead pastor or his designee. This is the natural outworking of all teams having a leader to which team members are accountable.

Our goal is to glorify God by functioning as a healthy Elder Council that works as a team and understands the need for leadership and accountability. We seek to be shaped functionally by the Gospel, which demands mutual submission, teamwork, accountability, service, and love.

The Story of the Bible

Many of the people we minister to do not understand the storyline of the Bible. They may know the Gospel and some of the major stories and characters of the Bible but do not have a grasp of how God's story flows through the sixty-six books of God's book. Not having this big picture is like trying to put the pieces of a puzzle together without having the overall image of the puzzle. Learning the skeleton story, in a simple and transferable way, allows those we are seeking to lead to build upon the story and add meat to the bone as they progress. Most important, knowing the storyline will make very clear why Jesus Christ came and why He is the theme of the Scriptures (John 5:39, Luke 24:44).

Outlined below is a way to share the message of the Bible in less than a minute and then in less than ten minutes.

Memorize this and share it with people. I have found it to be
both an excellent evangelistic and discipleship tool since most
people do not know the Bible's central message. Many times,
I have asked people who have shown an interest in the Gospel
if they would like to know the message of the Bible in less than
one minute. I have never been turned down, and several have
come to faith in Christ with this beginning. In addition, many
Christians do not know the storyline, and learning it provides
them a framework that will enable them to grasp God's purposes and how they fit into them.

THE STORY OF THE BIBLE IN LESS THAN ONE MINUTE:

The Bible's storyline can be summarized in four words: **Creation** (Genesis 1–2), **Fall** (Genesis 3), **Redemption** (Genesis
4—Revelation 18), **Restoration** (Revelation 19–22).

Once this basic outline is presented, a brief explanation of
each aspect can be amplified.

CREATION

God created everything good and made people in His image.
We were designed to have a love relationship with God. The
creation story is described in Genesis 1 and 2.

FALL

Adam and Eve chose to disobey God and go their own independent way, and fellowship with God was broken. They then
began to hide from God and each other and blame shift when
confronted with their rebellion. This sin is expressed in an

attitude of passive indifference to God or active rebellion. Genesis 3 tells the story.

REDEMPTION:

God is holy and can never overlook sin, yet He is love and longs to have a restored relationship with us. God made provision for our sin by providing a substitute: first, in the form of blood sacrifice and ultimately in Jesus Christ, God's Son, who lived a sinless life and then died in our place and rose from the dead. The story of God's redemptive plan is unfolded in the Bible from Genesis 4 through sixty-six books ending with Revelation 18.

RESTORATION:

Jesus Christ is coming back to judge and to restore fallen people and the fallen world. The new heaven and new earth that He will provide for us is described in Revelation 19–22.

THE STORY OF THE BIBLE IN LESS THAN TEN MINUTES.

Jesus Christ claimed to be the theme of the Old Testament Scriptures. He said to the religious leaders of his day, "You search the Scriptures because you think that in them you have eternal life; it is these that testify about Me" (John 5:39). After His resurrection from the dead, He taught two of his disciples, "These are my words which I spoke to you while I was still with you, that all things which are written about Me in the Law of Moses and the Prophets and the Psalms must be fulfilled" (Luke 24:44). He opened their minds to understand the Scriptures and said to them, "Thus it is written, that the Christ would suffer and rise again from the dead the third day." (Luke 24:44–46)

Understanding the basic storyline of the Bible will help you grasp and be able to articulate that the story of the Bible is about Jesus Christ.

God spoke all into existence for his glory, called it good, and assigned it order and purpose (Genesis 1–2). Now, as we walk through the story of the Bible, look for a series of two's which will help you easily remember the unfolding story.

TWO PROBLEMS:

Satan rebelled against God along with one third of the angels and established a counterfeit kingdom (Isaiah 14:12–15, Revelation 12:3–9). Adam and Eve rebelled against God, and as a result, they experienced spiritual death (Genesis 3).

TWO PURPOSES:

God purposed to redeem mankind and reclaim his kingdom. These two purposes are outlined in seed form in Genesis 3:15, 21, and 24. God's promised redemption and restoration will be fulfilled through His promised Messiah/Redeemer/King (John 5:39; Luke 24:27, 44–47).

TWO MEN:

God made a covenant with Abraham (2000 BC) and promised that though his seed/descendent all peoples would be blessed (Galatians 3:6–16). God made a covenant with King David of Israel (1000 BC) and promised that his descendent would establish His kingdom forever (Amos 9:12; Zechariah 14:9).

TWO MEASUREMENTS:

The first measurement, the law, is to show that we do not measure up to God's holy standards and we need a savior who will perfectly fulfill the standards for us. The second measurement is made up of the prophets who proclaimed prophecies about the coming Messiah—over sixty that had to be fulfilled in Him. The law, through Moses, demanded righteousness for those who would be redeemed (Exodus 20, Matthew 5:48). The prophets proclaimed that the Messiah/King would come and establish God's kingdom (Isaiah 9, 11; Daniel 2, 7).

TWO SONS:

Abraham's son Isaac *foreshadowed* the coming Redeemer (Genesis 22, John 1:29). He was going to be sacrificed, and God provided a substitute for him and promised one would come to pay for the sins of the world. David's son Solomon *foreshadowed* the coming King (1 Kings 10). Solomon was called the wisest man who ever lived; the nations flooded in with riches and paid homage to Him.

TWO ANIMALS:

The redemptive and kingdom functions of the coming Messiah are portrayed by two animals—the lamb and the lion. The sacrificial lamb typified Christ in his redemptive work (Isaiah 53:7, John 1:29). The lion, the king of beasts, typified Christ in his kingdom purposes (Genesis 49:9–10).

ONE REDEEMER AND KING:

Now we know why the New Testament opens the way it does in Matthew 1:1: "The record of the genealogy of Jesus the Messiah, the son of David, the son of Abraham." The genealogy demonstrates Jesus was the Messiah (predicted by the prophets) and is a descendant of David (fulfilling God's kingdom purposes) and of Abraham (fulfilling God's redemptive purposes).

No wonder Revelation 5:12 says, "Worthy is the lamb that was slain to receive power and riches and wisdom and might and honor and glory and blessing." We will worship Jesus Christ, Who fulfills God's two purposes—He redeemed us as the lamb that was slain in our place, and He reclaims His kingdom as the King of Kings and Lord of Lords.

Recommended
Resources

CHAPTER 1: CHECK YOUR FILTER

Knowing God by J. I. Packer (InterVarsity Press, 1973)

The Plan of God by J. I. Packer (Fig Books, 2012)

Desiring God: Meditations of a Christian Hedonist by John Piper (Multnomah, 1986)

The Pleasures of God by John Piper (Penguin RandomHouse, 2000)

The Holiness of God by R. C. Sproul (Tyndale, 2000)

The Existence and Attributes of God by Stephen Charnock (Baker Books, 1996)

21 Servants of Sovereign Joy by John Piper (Crossway, 2018)

CHAPTER 3: ALIGN YOUR LIFE

A Theology of the Church by Daniel Akin (B&H Publishing, 2014)

The Church: Sacraments, Worship, Ministry, Mission by Edmund P. Clowney (InterVarsity Press, 1995)

The Church: The Gospel Made Visible by Mark Dever (B&H Academic, 2012)

The Deliberate Church by Mark Dever and Paul Alexander (Crossway, 2005)

Systematic Theology: An Introduction to Biblical Doctrine, "Part 6: The Doctrine of the Church," by Wayne Grudem (Zondervan, 1994), pages 853–1049

Center Church: Doing Balanced, Gospel-Centered Ministry in Your City by Timothy Keller (Zondervan, 2012)

The Purpose Driven Church: Every Church is Big in God's Eyes by Rick Warren (Zondervan, 1995)

CHAPTER 4: LET THE GRACE OF GOD INSTRUCT YOU

Beyond Forgiveness: The Healing Touch of Church Discipline by Don Baker (Multnomah Books, 1984)

Guide to Church Discipline by Carl Laney (Bethany House Publishers, 1989)

Church Discipline: How the Church Protects the Name of Jesus by Jonathan Leeman (Crossway, 2012)

"Church Discipline: The Missing Mark" by Albert Mohler Jr, The Gospel Coalition, https://resources.thegospelcoalition. org/library/church-discipline-the-missing-mark

CHAPTER 8: DON'T LOSE HEART

Disappointment with God: Three Questions No One Asks Aloud by Philip Yancey (Zondervan, 1997)

Brokenness: How God Redeems Pain and Suffering by Lon Solomon (Red Door Press, 2005)

Emotionally Healthy Church: A Strategy for Discipleship That Actually Changes Lives by Peter Scazzero (Zondervan, 2015)

Bibliography

Barrett, Matthew, Schreiner, Thomas R., and VanDrunen, David. *The Five Solas Series*. Nashville: Zondervan, 2017.

Blackaby, Henry and Richard. *Spiritual Leadership*. Nashville: Broadman & Holman Publishers, 2001.

Butterfield, Rosaria Champagne. *The Secret Thoughts of an Unlikely Convert: An English Professor's Journey Into Christian Faith*. Pittsburgh: Crown & Covenant Publications, 2012.

Crossley, Robert. "Lowell and the History of Mars." *The Massachusetts Review* (Vol 41. No. 3), Autumn 2000.

Feldhahn, Shaunti. *The Good News about Marriage: Debunking Discouraging Myths About Marriage*. Colorado Springs: Multnomah, 2014.

Foster, Edward Halsey. *Susan and Anna Warner*. Woodbridge, Connecticut: Twayne Publishers, 1978.

Greear, J. D. *Gospel: Recovering the Power That Made Christianity Revolutionary*. Nashville: B&H Books, 2011.

Keller, Timothy. *Preaching: Communicating Faith in an Age of Skepticism*. New York: Viking, 2015.

Longhenry, Ethan R. *A Study of Denominations*. Chillicothe, Ohio: DeWard Publishing, 2015.

Packer, J. I. *The Plan of God*. Darlington: Evangelical Press, 1965.

Pei, Adrian. *The Minority Experience: Navigating Emotional and Organizational Realities*. Downers Grove, Illinois: IVP Books, 2018.

Piper, John. *21 Servants of Sovereign Joy: Faithful, Flawed and Fruitful*. Wheaton, Illinois: Crossway, 2018.

Piper, John. *God's Passion for His Glory: Living the Vision of Jonathan Edwards*. Wheaton, Illinois: Crossway, 2006.

Powlison, David. *Good and Angry: Redeeming Anger, Irritation, Complaining and Bitterness*. Greensboro, N.C.: New Growth Press, 2016.

Rainey, Dennis. *The Best Gift You Can Ever Give Your Parents*. Little Rock: FamilyLife, 2004.

Scazzero, Peter. *The Emotionally Healthy Church*. Nashville: Zondervan, 2005.

Serven, Doug, ed. *Heal Us, Emmanuel: A Call for Racial Reconciliation*. Oklahoma City: White Blackbird Books, 2016.

Shaw, Ed. *Same-Sex Attraction and the Church: The Surprising Plausibility of the Celibate Life*. Westmont, Illinois: InterVarsity Press, 2015).

Sweeney, Douglas A. *The American Evangelical Story: A History of the Movement*. Ada, Michigan: Baker Academic, 2005.

Wiersbe, Warren. *Meet Your Conscience*. Lincoln, Nebraska: Back to the Bible, 1983.

Wright, N. T. *The Resurrection of the Son of God*. Minneapolis: Fortress Press, 2003.

Yancey, Philip. *Disappointment with God*. Nashville: Zondervan, 1988.